THE POWER

OF DAD

The Influence Of Today's Fathers
And
The Destiny Of Their Children

BRIAN PRUITT

Dedication

This book is dedicated to my wife, Delicia, and my children, Brianna and Destiny. You are proof that the favor of God rests upon my life. As I have said so many times before, I say again, "You are the best thing that has ever happened to me." In you, God has given me more than I deserve. No sunset or sunrise can compete with the joy I find in your eyes. Every day I wake up to the love of a queen and two princesses. Thank you for loving me in my strengths and my weaknesses. I love you and I promise you will be blessed.

Special Thanks

Thanks to my beautiful wife Delicia Pruitt who is my constant co-author on every writing project that I venture to do.

To my mother Joyce Pruitt thank you for never giving up. Life must have been hard as a single parent mom. You are and forever will be my hero. I love you.

To my big sister Stephanie "The Champion" thanks for looking out for a little bad boy. You carried the weight for me as kids and I will never forget.

Thanks to my aunt Carolyn Pruitt for willingly being the editor for the books that God has placed within my heart. You are truly a blessing.

Even though I grew up fatherless throughout my life time God has always sent some awesome men to take me under their wings and mentor me. Since this book is written for men here are a few I would like to honor. These men taught me what it meant to have a positive influence on a child's destiny. These men taught me how to rightly use The Power of Dad.

Mike Mcmorris: I am not sure how you did it. You were a full time college student working a job and yet finding time to invest in an angry kid like me. The older I get the more awe I have for what you did. You have been a wonderful big brother and father figure. I love you. You taught me that it was ok to reach for the stars.

Lawrence McKinley: you have been a father to the fatherless for years. You have left a legacy of love, an example of responsibility, a shadow of servant-hood and gained many sons. I want you to know that the sacrifices that you have made will not go unrewarded. I love you dad!

Pastor James Glenn: Thanks for loving me unconditionally. You have been the constant model of what a Man of God should be. I only hope to grow up to be half the man, father and servant that you are. Words can not express my gratitude. The words that you have spoken into my life has propelled and projected me to unimaginable heights. You are my spiritual father. I love you.

Brian Molitor: You have been my extended family, friend and mentor. Thank you for calling me your own. You may not know this but I had never had a man refer to me as his son until I met you. Imagine being 18 years old and never have heard a father or male refer to you as (Son). It was that then foreign statement that began to release identity over my life.

Ron Ives you taught me character and integrity. You invested in me as your own. That weekly 5am prayer time with you taught me how to get on my knees and to fight for my future and my family. That weekly 5am bible study at J.W. Fillmore's taught me to study the word of God. My life to this day is built on these principals. Thank you. It is a blessing to know that my roots come form a man with such great passion for the things of God. I Love you.

Doug Carry: Over the years I have watched your life and family relationships. You are truly a man to be honored. The way you love your wife and children is unreal. You have been the model that I long to mirror in my own house. Thank you for your counsel on marriage, parenting and just being a man of God. You are one of my father figures. Your actions always line up and then speak louder than your words. I love you.

INTRODUCTION

Remember how excited you were when your child was first born? They came out screaming and the last thing you remember before the room started spinning and you passed out was thinking how blessed you were? Before you knew it, they were crawling across your floor and smiling at you and saying, "DA DA." That is short for dad.

Dad. It is a three letter word that will change your life. This word will bring you some wonderful times and some very painful times. If only that word, "Dad" came with an instruction manual. If it did, we, as men, would know exactly what to do to meet our children's every need, catching them before they fall. We would be seen as heroes in their eyes at all times. We only wish we had an instruction manual like that. Reality is, while millions of men have received the title "Dad," we are not, or were not, quite ready for the responsibility of being a dad. For the most part, we don't understand that dad is more than just a name. It is a place of responsibility. It is a place of God-given divine influence. How we use this influence will shape the destiny of the next generation of our family's history.

CHAPTER 1

What Is The Power of Dad?

My childhood best friend and I sat shedding tears as we had so many times before. My comforting session with my buddy always started and ended the same. His father would start out beating on his mom and then end his circus act with trying to dismantle his son. At times I wasn't sure what was more dangerous his anger or his drug problem. His father too often used damaging words like dumb, stupid and worthless. But I have to say that it was all the things that he never said that probably crushed his son the most. He seemed to possess an incredible talent to compare my buddy to every other kid in the neighborhood. Needless to say, his son never measured up. For years, like a master craftsman, I watched his daily criticisms chip away at the confidence of a very loving, talented and ambitious young man. Being around his father, let alone living with him, was like walking on eggshells. We never knew what would upset him. And, believe me it took very little to get him angry.

It was very common of my best friend to make negative comments about his father like:

"I hate him!"

"When I grow up I'm going to get him!"

And his ultimate statement of revenge: "I will never grow up to be like him!"

Yet underneath all the anger and resentment, you could see that all my friend wanted was to have a loving relationship with his hero, his father. Years went by and my buddy's situation only got worse. His mom finally got wise and left the abusive situation. I thought this was great because this seemed to be a way out for my pal. Because we went to the same high school, we still saw a lot of each other. What was wild was that even though my friend was not spending nearly as much time with his dad, it became clear that he had picked up a lot of his dad's characteristics. Slowly but surely I watched him migrate back to his father until he moved back into his father's house.

It wasn't long before my buddy had started a drug habit as well as becoming a womanizer. I will never forget the day that he told me how he and his dad were doing drugs. He even told me the story about how they went to a drug house. The place was so dangerous that his father gave him a gun and told him to stand guard at the front door. Even though he knew this was wrong, there he stood watching his father do drugs. He felt angry yet obligated to protect his hero. It was the approval of his dad that kept him at that door. Though his conscience pierced his very soul as to what he personally was becoming, his father's drug induced, glassy eyes nonverbally spoke words of affirmation that my friend always longed to hear. They said, "That's my son and I'm proud of him. Look at him being a man and watching his father's back!" That night he was perfect in his father's drug hazed eyes.

Since that memorable night, my friend has spent countless days in and out of jail for numerous reasons. Now when he looks in the mirror, whether he is in jail, after a domestic violence dispute, in some run down drug house, or in his son's eyes, he sees the reflecting image of his father.

What is the power of dad? It is the God-given influence that a father has to impact and set the course of his child's life. It is every man's choice how he uses that God-given influence. He can use it for the good of his children or for the bad. What we need to know about influence is that it never lies dormant. It is always being used by someone.

The Fear of Fatherhood

The bathroom door slammed open! My wife slowly came out with a smile as big as the sky and as bright as the sun. She was holding some little white stick and demanded that I take a look. I thought that I was in trouble for leaving dirty Q-tips in some inappropriate place leaving her to pick them up. Before I could give an explanation, my wife exclaimed, "It says I'm pregnant!" I was thinking how in the world could a Q-tip do that? I quickly realized that she was referring to the little stick that comes with a pregnancy test.

After telling me the good news, my wife stood in great expectation to see my reaction. I knew that this was a crucial moment and that I probably should say something loving and profound. I reached deep in to my archive of words for this very special moment. My wife kept waiting for what seemed like an eternity to hear my loving wise words. Finally I was confident with the response that I had chosen. So with all the Pruitt charm that I could muster, I pointed my finger at my wife and I said teasingly, "AH HA!" Startled by my response my wife said,

"What do you mean AH HA? Is that all you can say?" Needless to say she walked away upset. I was left standing there trying to pull my foot out of my mouth. My wife was upset the rest of the day.

I was just as excited to have a child as she was. After eight years of marriage we both were ready for children. Believe me I had always imagined that my response to that statement would be a lot different as well. However I never factored in the fear that would run through my heart. Most men fear one of four things prior to becoming a father:

(1) They will not be the great father that their dad was.
(2) They will be the bad father that their dad was, and their child will grow up feeling like they do about their dad.
(3) They have never had a father present in their lives, and they are eager to be what they never had. Yet, they haven't seen or even know the first thing about being a father.

(4) And finally, this is a big one: Could they be loved unconditionally despite their weaknesses? This one is the fear that
can be present in either of the second or third scenarios that
I just mentioned as well.

Do you remember when you and your wife first started dating
and how perfect you seemed in her eyes? You could do no wrong.
The further you fell in love the more she got to know you. It was
great until she found out that you were not perfect and that you had
flaws. Then you go through the issues that come with every relationship. Things like hurt, forgiveness, unforgiveness, tolerance, acceptance, rejection, and conflict. You both find out that you're human
and though you may love each other very much you still have to
work through issues like every one else. Our mates tend to put us up
on a pedestal only to remove and reinstate us on a regular basis.

I said all of this to say, could you imagine having a child who
grows up thinking that you're the best thing since sliced bread only
to come to the saving knowledge you are human. Just like your
marriage relationship, your parental relationship is going to have to
go through the same things: hurt, forgiveness, unforgiveness, tolerance, acceptance, rejection and conflict. You want to know the same
thing from your child as you wanted to know from your wife. That
is, will you love me when you find out that I'm only human? The
fearful part is we don't know the answer. Thus, we have incredible
divorce rates as well as a rift as large as the Atlantic Ocean forming
between parents and their children.

The Definition of Father

Webster's definition is pretty simple.
Father: The male parent, an ancestor, our fathers before us, an
originator (1).
I knew that Webster's definition was inadequate when I sat with
a young friend of mine who had just become a new father. Like
many men before him who had absent fathers, he was afraid of the
unknown. He feared all the mistakes he might make along the way

due to being uninformed and not having a role model. He wondered just how greatly his **involuntary ignorance** would eventually destroy his relationship with his own son. In trying to encourage him in his new role I asked him a vital question, and in return I received a haunting answer. That day I asked my young friend what was his definition of a father? His reply, "Someone you never want to grow up to be like. "

In hearing his definition, my mind quickly flashed back to a weekend I spent with a group of junior high students in the Smokey Mountains of Tennessee. After sharing my own personal story of my absent father, most kids in the room were becoming very transparent. I officially ended the meeting and offered the teens the opportunity to voluntarily stay behind to have a group discussion with me. To my surprise eighty percent of the teens wanted to stay and take part in the discussion. We sat in a circle and they began to pour their hearts out. They told stories of fathers who they hadn't talked to in several years. What's even sadder, some of the dads only lived a few blocks down the street from them. There were also discussions of fathers whose love was conditional, who couldn't control their anger, and how their children were afraid of them. In addition, there were stories of fathers who were dealing with so much hurt from their own childhood that they couldn't rise up to be dads for their children.

Although the teens felt their situations were hopeless, it became very clear that regardless of their dads' shortcomings, they still longed for their father's love.

At the end of the session I asked each kid to share his or her biggest fear in life regarding their father. Depending on the gender, the answer was different but consistent. Most boys feared that they would grow up to be like their fathers. While most girls feared they would grow up to marry someone like their dad.

I'm sorry to say it but there is not a man in the world that could receive a right perspective on what it really means to be a father from Webster's definition. It's no longer good enough to just be the male parent, an ancestor or originator. On the other hand, there is much to learn from the definition that we get from America's youth.

Our sons are demanding that we be someone that they want to grow up to be like again. Our daughters are demanding that we be the standard for the men that they will marry.

Your child needs you! Can you work through the issues you have with your own father enough to rise up and be the father you always said you would be to your kids? Most of us have said it before:

"When I grow up I'm not going to treat my kids like that!"
"When I grow up I'm not going to say hurtful things to my kid like that!"
"I'm not going to ignore my kids like that!"
"I'm not going to let anger destroy my family like that."
"I'm going to love my kids unconditionally!"

Well, if you haven't noticed, you're all grown up now! Time is ticking away. Your child is waiting. Although you may think that it's too late to make up for lost time, I say it's too crucial not to make up for lost time. One thing is for sure, in a year from now you and your child's relationship will either be better or worse. I'm not saying that he/she will respond right away but I am saying that eventually your child will respond. The initial response may be one of bitterness, unforgiveness, anger or just being very closed. Eventually the innate desire of kids to be loved by their father will surface. This is when the relationship you always wanted begins. You didn't get into this situation overnight, and you may not get out of it overnight. Go into this battle being prepared to fight for your legacy, your child. In ending let me ask, WHAT IS YOUR DEFINITION OF A FATHER?

Fatherlessness

It was Thursday afternoon. I just finished a major project that I had been working on for the past three weeks. My mind was tired and my body was screaming for a time out. After a nice cold shower and a pleasant hot lunch, I was ready to spend the day in a little relaxation. I decided that I would start my make-shift vacation out by watching some TV. While flipping through the channels looking for something interesting, I came across the Maury Povich Talk Show. I'm not big on watching talk shows; however it was the topic that caught my attention. Maury did a show that day on fathers. He said that his main objective was to help young women find their children's fathers.

After a quick commercial break the show got started. Maury in his witty television-talk-show voice introduced the show's first guest. As she took the stage, you could see that the pain within her heart was so great it seemed to cause her to walk with a limp. Not a physical limp but a limp of insecurity, low self-esteem and shame. You see many young women with this limp. It has been developed, inflicted and or caused at times by their bad judgment in men.

Maury revealed that one of the five guests appearing on the show was her child's father. When she heard this, she sheepishly smiled. She sat down slowly with great expectation of the live audience condemning her with their words. Just as she had expected, like large stones being forcibly projected toward fragile glass, their demising chants started. As she fought back tears and tried to gain her composure, Maury pointed toward a large screen. Immediately a huge image of an eight-year-old boy came up on the monitor. His boyish smile caused the crowd to simultaneously gasp for air. In his eyes was the look of excitement. He was on national television! Not knowing why he was America's interest, there was also a look of total confusion.

After a quite lengthy commercial break, Maury began to introduce the five men. Dance music started playing and the crowd started clapping to the beat in unison. Each young man came dancing out onto the stage. With every rhythmic move of their body, they each chanted, "The kid is not my son!" Right away I recognized the statement as lyrics from a song called "Billy Jean" that was made famous by Michael Jackson.

As the young men took their seats, the young lady in rage tried to attack them yelling, "One of you are my son's father!" After Maury got the young lady calmed down he called for the results of the DNA test. The cameras quickly took a shot of her face. She was biting her lip nervously; there was a look of hope in her eyes. Then the camera took close up shots of the faces of the young men on stage. Every one of them was staring at the large image of the eight year old on the screen behind them. Even though they were laughing and having a good time, they all got very serious at this moment. They were intently looking at the little boy. With x-ray eyes they looked him over to see if there was any similar attributes between them and the eight year old. Some of them decided that the boy didn't look like them. They took deep sighs of relief and then continued to act foolishly with confidence. Others who noticed some physical similarities began to sweat profusely and found it hard to sit still.

To build the intensity of the show Maury said that the truth would be revealed after a brief commercial break. After promotions of dish detergents, baby pampers and beer, the show came back on. Maury asked the participants if they were ready to find out the test results. They all fretfully answered yes.

Slowly the test results were opened. One by one he gave each prospect an answer. The first young man jumped to his feet with a shout upon hearing he was not the father. The young lady still sat there in full confidence that her son's father was in the building. The second gentleman was so ecstatic that he ran and jumped in the young lady's face and with a smile said, "I told you that boy wasn't mine!" The third fellow sat impatiently ringing his hands. However the answer he received was worth his wait. His test results were also negative. Falling out of his chair to his knees, he screamed at the top of his lungs, "Yes Lord!" He preceded this comment by hurling insults at the little boy's mother.

Of course these were words that had to be bleeped out.

By now the young lady was in tears. She didn't look nearly as confident about finding her son's father as she did a few minutes ago. However, there were still two test results to be disclosed. The fourth guy sat in his seat with his face in his hands. It was pretty obvious that he was praying. There were only two men left, which meant the likelihood of him being the father was very high. The test results were given. He was not the father! Shouting, "I'm the man!" He acted as if he had just hit the winning shot in a basketball game. At this point in the show the woman was on her feet crying and screaming obscenities at the five men. Shame was overtaking her. With each test result the embarrassment was becoming too much for her to bear.

Finally the last result was to be given. The crowd began taunting the last man assuming that since he was the only one left, he had to be the father. The tears that were running down his face confirmed that he had come to the same conclusion. The other four young men were having what looked like a party and joining in on the taunting of the last prospect.

Finally the last test result was revealed. After hearing the results within a matter of seconds the room became totally silent. There was a sense of total disbelief. The results came back negative on the fifth gentleman as well. The young lady dropped to her knees in anguish. Almost simultaneously the young man jumped out of his seat throwing his hands in the air in pure joy. He ran and leaped into the arms of the four other men. He looked as if he had won the super bowl in double overtime with a last second field goal.

Suddenly the taunts of the audience were now being directed toward the young lady. Those who felt they were without sin were eager to cast the first stones. Each insult came with its own sting of condemnation. Her child's father was still somewhere out there. She had never had a great relationship with her own father and obviously spent the majority of her life looking for approval and love from various men. As Maury helped her stand to her feet she repeatedly stated that her son didn't need a father and that she could raise him herself. Yet it was clear that she was devastated not to mention embarrassed.

It was bizarre! The men didn't care that this kid was watching them rejoice over the fact that neither of them were his father. Not to mention the mother who was more concerned about herself than her child. It was all about them! None of them thought about the fact that this one-hour talk show would be etched in the mind of this little boy forever.

As the show came to an end dance music started playing and the crowd started clapping to the beat in unison. Each young man started dancing his way off the stage. Again with every rhythmical move of their body they each chanted, "The kid is not my son!" As the young lady exited the stage I couldn't help but to notice that her limp had gotten worse. The last camera shot of the show was of the little boy. Without a care in the world he just sat in the background on the big screen playing with a little truck. Although his mother said that he didn't need a father I couldn't help but wonder how old he would be before he disagreed with her statement.

This young man, like over 24 million other youth, will live absent of his biological father. Sometimes that means that their dad is physically not there and other times that he is mentally not there. At all times this means that there is a fatherless generation that is larger than the state of Texas by one million people. Envision a city of over 24 million fatherless youth. Could you imagine the chaos, lack of purpose, violent acts, missing morals, deficient identities and the decay of society? Just the thought of it is scary enough to make you think of Judgment Day.

Well I've got news for you. D-Day is here and this society exists, over 24 million and growing. If 24 million teens came down with a case of chickenpox, the flu or even diarrhea for that matter, our country would interrupt every scheduled program on our television sets and declare it a state of emergency.

According to 72% of the U.S. population, fatherlessness is the most significant family or social problem facing America. Like the young men on the Maury Povich show we have denied our responsibility of being fathers and danced our way off stage.

We as men have excused ourselves from the biggest battle of all time.

The battle for the next generation. The battle for our kids.

Education In Broken Hearted Youth Hearts Don't Lie

He stared at me with glaring eyes. I wasn't sure why he didn't like me but it was very clear that he didn't. As I continued telling my personal story of fatherlessness to three hundred teens, he became more and more restless. It wasn't unusual to see a young person do this while I was speaking, especially if I was speaking of areas they could relate to. What was unusual was how abruptly he got out of his seat. He shoved several students rudely to the side, made his way to the back door, and in anger slammed it behind him. I must say I had never seen someone do that before. However, every time I speak I like to think of it as getting an education in brokenhearted youth. So I am always ready to learn something new.

Every teen in the room was totally distracted. I knew that it was my job as the speaker to try to get their attention back on me. Several minuets passed and the crowd calmed down. Strangely enough, I noticed that no one went to check on the young man who had walked out of the door. As I came to the end of my speech the back door slammed open. Once again the crowd's attention went immediately to the back of the room. I was standing at the front of the room wondering why one of the adult leaders wasn't handling the situation.

As the young man walked up the aisle, I assumed that he would make a detour and head back to his seat. I was wrong! He was heading toward me! His fists were clinched, face was drenched in sweat, and eyes bloodshot. His anger was blowing like bellows of smoke from a run away train. At that moment I have to say that my concern was no longer for him. I was more worried about my own safety. The room became very silent. It seemed as if everyone knew something about this kid and his violent history but me. While I was not sure of his acts of violence from the past I was sure that his legend was going to stop with me. Taking into mind that the leaders at the retreat did not intervene and that the young man was large in stature I was ready to do whatever it took to defend myself.

There we were staring at each other face to face, eye to eye. I was just waiting for him to make his move so that I could legally call my actions self defense. Right in the midst of me thinking of how I was going to restrain this young man, I noticed that he wasn't sweating profusely but that he was drenched in his own tears. Slowly he unclenched his fists and dropped to his knees. With his arms wrapped around my waist, he repeatedly cried out, "Why doesn't he love me?" It didn't take long for me to realize that he was talking about his father.

At that moment the crowd let out a big sigh of relief. There was not going to be a big brawl after all. Astonishingly, teens throughout the entire room started leaving their seats and joined us at the front of the room. From each teens eyes tears began to fall as hard and fast as any rainfall I'd ever seen. The sounds of their now unmuted cries rolled through the room like thunder. It was an unbearable moment. All I could do was hold as many teens in my arms as I could and cry with them. It was a sobering reminder that hearts don't lie. And the hearts of America's youth are saying, "Dad I'm hurting and I need you."

CHAPTER 2

Powerful ROOTS!

Deja Vu

It was a reoccurring nightmare! Generation after generation of intelligent and talented men in my family fell prey to the same flaws of anger and physical abuse. Each one of them suffered unspeakable violence at the hand of their father. I can imagine they all heard the loud arguments in the night. They likely snuck around the corner to see what was going on and watched their mothers receive physical beatings that not even a pro boxer could withstand. As they watched they were overwhelmed with emotions. They felt helpless, because they couldn't stop what was happening to their family. They felt fearful, because they knew that the rage in their father's hearts would soon turn toward them. The next morning they would awake to the smell of bacon, biscuits and eggs. As they rushed out to the breakfast table they would undoubtedly notice the bad jobs their mothers did at hiding hideous bruises with makeup. Vowing in their hearts to be different, love their wives, and bless their children, each one failed.

The tradition continued for four generations.

My Four Fathers

Forefathers: A person who is from an earlier time and has contributed to a common tradition shared by a particular group. My forefathers contributed to a common tradition of violence!

Great Grandfather

Old Blue was my great grandfather. He was given the name Old Blue by his family. What's most interesting is how he acquired this name. He was a tall, well built man, from the south. He was raised by farmers who were slaves. At that time in the south, a black man didn't have many rights, didn't own very much, and had little authority. His home was the one place where he was the king of the castle.

Let me give you some history about Old Blue. Old Blue grew up in a tough home. Blue's father daily received criticism, demeaning words, and if he wasn't careful, physical abuse at work. By the time he got home he was ready for some due respect. Blue, his siblings, and mom all had to greet the king of the castle properly as he entered the house. The manly ego that had been crushed all day at work was now ready to be stroked. He was motivated all day long through fear and intimidation. When he got home to his own castle he ruled it the same way.

Even though he was not a well-educated man, Blue thought that his father knew everything. Time proved that the one thing he didn't know was with every form of abuse, he was shaping the character of his son and leaving a legacy that would curse his offspring for generations.

Finally Blue got the courage to leave home and start his own life. He eventually married a beautiful girl and had children. No longer a little boy taking beatings and standing by helplessly while his mom and siblings lived in fear, **he was now a man who carried on his father's flaws.** All the years of pain, anger and frustration were now unleashed upon his wife and kids.

Old Blue was the type of man who could physically protect his family from outside dangers. The only problem was that he was the only one bringing harm to his family. He couldn't seem to protect them from himself. Blue never tried to hide his bad temper. My great grandfather never suffered at the slave owner's hands. He suffered from the slave mentality that his father had bought into. His father used outrageous forms of discipline that he learned from slave masters. Blue also used these methods of discipline. This is where he got his name. He was known for physically beating his wife and children which left them black and blue. So the name Blue was given to him by his family, not out of honor, but out of shame.

Let me ask you some questions. What does your family call you and why? Have you mastered the art of protecting them from the hurt and harm of the outside world? Most important: **have you learned to protect them from you**?

Grandfathers

In the bible, Samson was one of the strongest people of his time. He was given this strength to judge and protect his people and family. However, because of his inability to control himself, he not only lost his strength, he lost his life.

Samson would have been a better name for my grandfather, David, Blue's eldest son. He was a man of incredible physical strength. It was very common for people to stand in awe of my grandfather's physique. But, like Samson, what was more impressive than his physical strength was his lack of self-control.

David's third grade education was hidden well behind his PhD from the school of hard knocks. The abuse that he suffered from his father's hands was only one of many reasons that he left home at an early age. One would think that his lack of education along with his youthful age would have been a great disadvantage in dealing with a ruthless world. However, David not only had the strength of ten men but the work ethic as well. What he couldn't write or read on paper, he could build with his hands. If he could visualize it in his mind he could pull a group of men together to make it a reality.

My grandfather's quality work gained him a great reputation and allowed him to eventually start his own construction business. Many said that it was the love of his life, but it wasn't.

As pretty as her name, my grandmother, Rose, stole David's heart at first sight. But like any rose not taken care of properly, their petals fall and their beauty is to be seen no more. The story you're about to hear is one of true tragedy. While every detail can not be discussed in its entirety, I will share this story with you as it has been passed down to me.

It was the ageless story of boy meets girl. Although they were young they knew that they wanted to be together. So they naturally took the next step and got married. For my grandfather, Rose was his first love and his opportunity to prove that he could be a better man than Old Blue. And for my grandmother, David was a knight in shinning armor that would soon lose his shine.

Over the next few years they had four children. Due to the poor job market, my grandparents moved their family to Michigan. David learned early in his marriage that being a better man than his father was not going to be as easy as he thought. The curse of anger and abuse seemed to haunt him daily. Like his father, he found himself beating his children in unusual ways and using his wife as a punching bag. He watched his kids peek their eyes through cracked doors as they watched their mother fall to the floor in convulsions due to heavy blows to the head. Hours later after Rose had gathered enough strength to get back to her feet she would stumble her way toward the cries coming from the back room where the kids slept. When she would open the door, her four children would mob and adorn her with affection as if she had come back from the dead.

On the other side of the house, David locked himself behind closed doors. Listening to the agonizing sounds of his wife peeling herself off the floor, he would breathe a sigh of relief that she was still alive. He would hear my grandmother slowly limp her way toward the children's room to give and receive comfort. And in his moment of shame and self-condemnation he would realize once again that he was walking in the footsteps of his father. For David this scene was all too familiar. He lived it as a child and now as a man he had come to the bitter discovery of just how powerful his father's influence was on his life. During moments like this my grandpa's **childhood pain and manhood frustrations** would turn into a cry that was evident of his inner torment. My grandfather could build anything but a family. It was, by far, his most challenging building project, and most of its weakness came from the fact that the foundation wasn't poured correctly.

My grandmother would soon find out that she had a thing for picking men who had bad foundations. Finally, tired of being beaten into seizures and watching her children live in fear. Rose made a decision that she thought would better her life. Grandma courageously packed her things and escaped with her children.

Now I'm not sure how it happened. Somehow in the midst of this domestic mess between my grandparents, another man entered into the picture. Much like David he was a knight in everything but shinning armor. His name was Caesar. Unlike David who was more of a blue-collar workhorse, Caesar was a smooth, ladies man. By the time he met my grandmother she was a young lady who was tired, beat up and struggling with her own self worth. Most of all, she was a young woman who just wanted to be treated like the rose she was. Knowing that my grandmother was a married woman seemed to just add to the challenge of winning her over. For Caesar women were trophies, and he wanted to add Rose to his accolade of awards. She quickly became a pawn between two very competitive forces.

Caesar left his wife; my grandmother, her husband. Soon afterwards they married and started their new life. In a twist of strange events, like something from a soap opera, to spite Caesar, my grandfather began to date and then married Caesar's ex-wife. Caesar inherited my grandfather's wife and children; my grandfather inherited Caesar's wife and children. While living in the same city, my grandfather and Caesar became the worst of enemies. This was as exciting as the Hatfield's and McCoy's. It was an eye-for-an-eye, tooth-for-tooth, and wife-for-wife relationship. The future held many threats and attempts of murder. To those who knew of this wild situation, it was no surprise when someone was murdered. What was most surprising was who got murdered.

Like a fugitive on the run she packed her bags once again to flee a prison of abuse. Grandma had finally given up hope of finding true love. Her time spent with Caesar only proved that she spent too many years afflicted by domestic violence. Sure it came in many different outward appearances, but none the less it was violence. When she was younger she was blinded by his flattering words, masculine smell of cologne, and visions of love. However, he never failed to unveil himself by greeting her with a surprise of heavy punches to the head.

Run though she may, Rose would soon gain the courage to face her adversary.

The Motor City seemed to be the perfect camouflage for grandma to hide her family from Caesar and David. For the first time in years, there was no man to answer to and no bruises to hide. Rose and the children were free to be themselves. Laughter filled the halls. Grandma's days were spent working hard to provide for her family. When she arrived home she would cook dinner with the expertise of a gourmet chef. At night, she listened to her children share their personal dreams. Like a loving mother she made them believe that nothing was impossible. As good as it was, little did they know that this was only the calm before the storm.

The night the storm blew in will never be forgotten. Grandma went about her normal daily routine, spending the day working hard and thanking God for her loving talented children. Upon getting home she began cooking one of the kid's favorite meals. Her youngest child, excited to see her home, decided to use mom as a jungle gym. So as she cooked he wrapped himself around her leg playfully.

When grandma finished, she yelled to the kids to clean up and come to the dinner table. Each family member took their seat and traditionally joined hands in prayer before partaking in their well-prepared meal. As their prayer time was coming to an end they couldn't help but to notice the sound of the squeaky back door opening. Because all the family members were already at the dinner table they ignored the sound. Although every eye was closed and every head was bowed in prayer, they felt an evil presence enter into the room. The atmosphere changed. The smell of grandma's home cooking was drowned out by the familiar stench of old cologne and malt liquor. Just the scent began to bring back bad memories that caused chills to go up and down their spines. Anxiety began to over take a very peaceful family moment. As Rose ended her prayer by saying, "In Jesus name amen." There was a moment of silence, while they contemplated the terror before them.

When they opened their eyes their vision was somewhat blurred. However, they all could see the distorted view of an uninvited guest. There he stood, eyes blazing red with evil intentions in his heart, a sinister smile on his face, and a shotgun clinched loosely in one hand. It was Caesar! His rage had compelled him to spend a number of months trying to track my grandmother down like a dog. He had finally found her, and now he was going to make her pay. No one was going to leave him unless he said they could leave and Caesar had not given his permission. Not to mention he feared that Rose would return to my grandfather and that would mean Caesar would have lost everything to him. There was no way he was going to let this happen. Grandma was his property which meant more to him than her being his wife.

Tired of running, grandma told the kids to go to the bathroom. They obeyed. All four children were packed like sardines in the small space. The oldest child, my father, put his arms around the other three while they waited and listened. Through the paper-thin, offset bath-room door they heard Caesar say, "You are going to learn!" At the flick of his wrist, the shotgun swung upwards and then towards my grandmother. With the barrel of the shotgun pointed at her head, her life began to flash before her eyes. I'm sure she thought of precious childhood moments, and what her children would grow up to be. She didn't want to spend the rest of her life running. So like she did so many times before, she defied all the odds. Grandma looked at Caesar, David, and every obstacle that she had overcome up to this point in her life and with all confidence and said, "You don't want to do that!" As if she was telling him, "If you miss I won't!" Cesar's reply was, "Yes I do!" He slowly twitched his finger and BOOM! The bathroom walls shook. The sound of flesh, blood and bone sounded like a hard rainstorm splashing on a tin roof. The chil-dren huddled tightly and clinched their fist as if they had braced themselves for a car accident. As the youngest child screamed the eldest clinched her mouth shut firmly with his hand. He knew that they would be next to die if any attention was brought to them. After all Caesar had nothing left to lose. They waited in fear as they heard footsteps on the other side of the door. Their hearts were pounding like a drum until they noticed that the footsteps were growing faint instead of louder. He was leaving.

As they heard the door close, the car start and speed away, they breathed a sigh of relief. They opened the door to the bathroom slowly. There was blood, flesh and bone all over the walls. In a panic they began to call for their mother. There was no reply. They looked down in the corner of the room and there she was. The children fell to their knees and gathered around her. Just then, a close relative showed up and was shocked by the scene. In an unwise spontaneous decision, they commanded the kids to help clean the mess up. So one by one they began to clean her shattered remains. I can only imagine my father cleaning his mother's blood off the walls and floor and vowing that when he grew up he would never be like David or Caesar. But time would only tell just how powerful the influence of his dad and step dad would be.

Father

Years later, my father still carries that haunting image in his mind. He quickly forgot about the vow that he made to himself that night. My dad grew up and gave way to the curse of his grandfather, father and stepfather. Slowly he became the main character in his own nightmare and for the fourth generation violence ruled. He beat the women he loved, and abandoned the children he had.

My father, James, spent a lifetime of watching men act like little boys. His father or stepfather never gave him the love or the example of manhood that he needed. David, his father, who was a construction worker; he wanted my dad to follow in his footsteps. My granddad never accepted the fact that his son was an incredible artist and needed to be respected and supported in his trade. Instead he degraded him because he was different. The truth was both were artist; they both worked with their hands and created things. My granddad didn't see it that way. He made it very clear how disappointing my father was to him. In regards to Caesar, his step dad. He never spent one day in prison for the murder of my grandmother and he never loved my father like he was his own. James was his stepson and that's all that he would ever be. Caesar always made my father feel as if he was the male version of Cinderella. However in his story, there was no happy ending. He was left with a family in mourning for their slain mother.

As much as my heart goes out to my father for the things that he experienced, I still needed him. Needed him to do what?

I needed him to rise from the ashes of his life and use his power or influence as a dad to protect me from the hurts of this world.

I needed him to be there just to say that I was his son and he was proud of me.

I needed him to show me how to go from being a boy into a man.

Now I respectfully know that my expectation was not unreasonable but maybe unrealistic. I now know that I was asking all of this from **a hurt little boy that I called dad.**

Sometimes the hurt little boy in us never lets us grow up to be the man we want to be. You're a grown man but you still:

-throw fits like a little boy

-have not learned to control the anger of the little boy

-want your father's love

-wonder why he did what he did

-wonder where did he go

-wonder why am I not good enough

-haven't learned that punching walls only hurts you; the wall doesn't care

-make decisions with the poor insight of a little boy

-have not learned to have a deep conversation

-have not learned to passionately love or to give to others until it hurts.

Wondering why everybody keeps expecting adult things from you when you're just a little boy trapped in an adult's body.

Think about your ancestors. What was the struggle for the men of your family? If you don't know, ask your relatives. As men and fathers, many of our personal struggles are received and passed down from generation to generation until it is recognized and dealt with.

CHAPTER 3

Powerful Memories, Mirrors & Mentors

Memories — My Story

I was six years old when I found out what a dad was. I guess I never thought about it before then. I spent the next sixteen years of my life wondering where my father was. From age six to twenty-two I experienced the power of an "absent dad." Night after night I asked myself, "How is it possible that my father doesn't care what I look like?" I vividly remember the day when I started asking myself this question.

I'm not sure which caught my eye the most on that sunny day. It may have been the unfamiliar glow of expectation in my sister's eyes or the rapid knock on the door that announced the entrance of her father. As this tall handsome man came through the door, my sister sprinted towards him and jumped into his arms. With more joy than any Olympic sprinter who had just won a gold medal, she yelled, "Daddy!" He embraced her tightly and spun her in a circle.

Without a thought, I began to run towards her dad. Suddenly I felt something grab my shirt. The next few steps I took felt as if I was pulling a trailer that weighed a thousand pounds. I was not discouraged. I just swung my arms harder, kicked my legs faster, and yelled the foreign word," daddy!" Just then, I noticed that I was being pulled backwards. The sound of my mother's voice saying,

"No honey!" made me realize that she was pulling me back to her side.

My sister and her father slowly turned, waved goodbye, and headed out the door hand in hand. My mom and I watched this awesome reunion; they seemed to cherish every moment. This was a relationship that my sister greatly needed. It also was a relationship that would come to a screeching halt just a few years later when my sister's father was found murdered. I'll never forget how the news devastated her. It was like a wrecking ball hit a tall strong building leaving piles of rubbish behind for blocks. And though we all cared, no one knew how to put her back together again. The damage was too great, too deep, and too extensive. She was never the same after that. He was gone, and his daughter needed him.

As the door closed shut that day, the room was filled with silence. At that moment, three questions stormed my six year old mind. First, with much curiosity I asked my mom," Who was that man?" She promptly answered, "He's your sister's dad. Not yours." This explained why she pulled me back. I did not belong to him, and he had not come to visit me. Secondly, I asked my mom," Who is my dad?" She reluctantly mentioned his name. Her facial expressions showed pain from bad memories she'd rather forget. Finally I asked her," Where is he?" She took a long pause, lovingly put her hands around my face, and said, "I don't know." At that moment I was enraged and ran upstairs to my room. As I sat and cried, feelings of anger, rejection and abandonment overwhelmed me. My grief over my fatherlessness changed me. My esteem shrunk and my self-value began to erode away. I wanted to know who was my dad! Why did he leave me? Did he love me? Doesn't he even care what I look like?

From that moment I began to get into a lot trouble. I got into numerous fights and spent many days kicked out of school. I would unleash my anger on whomever and wherever I could. I was hurt and I wanted others to hurt. I wounded the people I loved; I tried to destroy the people I despised. It's funny now, but I made the incredible hulk my role model. I loved the way he would stop his pain by releasing so much anger that he would turn green, put on fifty pounds of muscle, and destroy everything in his path. Of course later, he would calm down and have no memory of what he had done. I lived life by one rule; I could not be held responsible for my actions when I lost my temper. This seemed to work out just fine for the Hulk. There never seemed to be any consequences. Or was there?

The Hulk was really a man by the name of David Banner. He wandered from town to town blowing up on people who upset him. He always gave a warning by simply saying, "You won't like me when I'm angry!" Then he would explode into a fit of rage. In all the years I watched the Hulk, he was never able to fall in love or build a relationship with the people he cared for. Why? He was a man who could not control his anger. He was always afraid of what he might do to them. He had no self-control. This left him a very lonely man wandering the streets of America. He looked for someone who could help him control his anger so that he could live, learn, love and just be David. Strangely enough, the Hulk was a lot like my great grandfather, grandfather, father, and sorry to say, me.

The Man In The Mirror

It was another year of Father's Day celebrations, and I continued in my annual Father's Day tradition. It was a well thought-out plan. The night before this national holiday I would hang out in the streets until I was exhausted. My goal was to make sure that I would be so tired that I would sleep right through Father's Day. As well constructed as my plan was, it never seemed to work. Without fail by noon a painful internal alarm would go off. Ringing louder than any physical alarm clock, it gave off unbearable feelings of rejection and abandonment. The pain that I felt in my heart would then cause me to toss and turn for the next twenty minutes. Knowing that there was no snooze button to shut it off, I tried to drown it out. I was willing to try anything to stop this painful, emotional alarm clock from going off. I attempted everything from putting my pillow over my head, to turning on the radio and the television, and sometimes at the same time. Immediately I would be bombarded with movies and TV shows, all singing the praises of men on their celebrated day. After a while I would combat the pain with my anger. I would go into fits of rage that would land me on the floor of my room in tears. I am not proud to say it. But I almost became a part of the 63% of fatherless youth who attempt suicide. Like them I wanted to be free of the pain even if it meant death. To me, Father's Day was just a twenty-four hour reminder of how unimportant I was. Eventually I would pull myself together and spend the rest of the day letting the world know that I was in a bad mood. I was hurt and I wanted everyone, even the people that I loved most, to hurt with me.

My mother had the hardest times with me during this time. In my anger I emotionally pushed her away and blocked her out. However everything within me was screaming for her to come and hold me. I wanted her to make the pain go away like she had done so many other times before when I was a child. Yet I would not let her comfort me. I was confused and chose to deal with things my own way. The power or influence of my dad was killing me. I never wanted to let her know that I could be so hurt by my father. I never wanted her to know that there were nights that I longed for him. I always thought that it would belittle everything that she had done for me. I never wanted to hurt her, but I did!

After a day of intense thought on the absence of my father and rehearsing how much I hated and loved him, I was emotionally drained. My mother and I began to engage in what seemed to be a promising conversation. My mom mentioned that I had forgotten to take out the trash. Instead of just doing it, I snapped! We went from having a good conversation to me screaming at the top of my lungs within a matter of seconds. It was bigger than the chores. I was emotionally spent, and this was the beginning of an emotional breakdown for me. I went into a rage and all of a sudden taking the garbage out didn't seem so important any more. Screaming profanities, gritting my teeth, clinching my fist tight, stomping through the house, and turning over everything in my way, I raged against the world that day.

My mother asked me what was wrong. She tried to grab me by my arm. I yelled hurtful things at her and ran to the front of the house. I felt like a caged animal trying to get free. As I headed towards the front door, I had no intention of opening it. I punched it. I punched it as if it was everything and any body that had ever caused me pain. Instantly a crack ran down the middle of a solid oak hardwood door. From the top to the middle of the door, day light broke through. You could see the outside, from the inside. As I stood there in awe of the awesome feat of strength I had just performed. I heard my mother behind me crying. With my fists still clinched, tears flowing, and heart racing with rage, I slowly turned. There she was on her knees and in tears. She said, "Go ahead and hit me." Stunned and stuttering, I asked her what was she talking about? Again she said, "Go ahead and hit me. You know that's what you want to do!" She pointed her finger at me and made a statement that I will never forget. With great disappointment she said, "You're just like your father!" It was the most depressing and sobering thing I had ever heard. My mom had never said anything like that to me before. She tried to raise me to be a better man than my dad. As much as I wanted to deny her accusations I couldn't. There my mother was on her knees crying.

The house was torn to pieces. The door was cracked in two pieces. My mother became a mirror that I could see myself in. It gave off a reflection of a young man who had the same rage in his heart as his forefathers. That day I saw and met my father for the first time. I seemed to know more about him in that moment than at any other time in my life. It brought a new meaning to the phrase, "You look just like your father." People said that to me so often, and I hated it because I had no idea what he looked like. However that day his image was very clear in the (mirror) reflection of my mother's brokenness and pain. I saw his eyes red with rage, face aged with expressions of anger, muscles pulsating with no intent to hold back their wrath. I felt his heart beating at a pace that not even the world's best drum line could maintain. Without missing a beat my heart pumped pain through my veins. The sight that was before me combined with my emotional state caused fear to grip me. I feared the man in the mirror. I screamed out in desperation to shatter the image. I felt as if this hideous reflection was drowning me by forcing my very person under deep waters. To make matters worse, it seemed that I had no strength left to fight for my last gasp of breath. I had met my match. The man in the mirror was bigger, stronger and winning!

Not knowing what else to do, I grabbed my car keys and headed towards the door. The sound of the rattling keys caused my mother to jump to her feet. I was in no shape to drive. She tried to stop me from leaving the house without success. Once I made it to the car, I sped out of my driveway. I was running! Running from the man in the mirror!. Running from my father! Running from my self. Running scared!

That day I learned that mirrors are reflective; they show us what we look like and who we are. I've learned that there are situations in life that also act as mirrors which allow us to see ourselves. Through seeing a true reflection of ourselves through these mirrors, we then have the opportunity to make a decision to change what we see in that mirror or to remain the same.

As men we have similar mirrors in our lives. For example:

1. Adversity
   The hard times tell you who you truly are.
   Are you a man of integrity?
   Will you do anything to get out of a tough situation?
   Who have you hurt because of your pain during this time?

2. Success
   How did you become successful?
   Did you step on others to make it to the top?
   What do you do to maintain your success?
   If you lost your success, would your life still be complete?
   Without mentioning your success, how would you describe
      yourself?

3. Wives/significant others/children
   How do you treat them?
   How would they describe you as a person?
   Am I a good example of what a husband should be for my
      son or daughter?

4. Friends
   How did you choose them?
   Who did you choose? (Birds of a feather flock together)

5. Finances
   How do you use them?
   Do you help others or only yourself and family?
   Do you save or invest for the future?
   Are you financially stable or have a lot of debt?

6. Purpose
   Do you know your purpose?
   Do you have goals?
   Do you have plans to accomplish your goals?
   What excuses do you make when your goals are not met?

7. Privacy
   What do you do when no one else is looking?

8. God's Word
   Do you read it?
   Do you know what you believe?
   How do you apply it?
   How often do you lead your family to God's house!
   (Church)

Think about all of the situations or mirrors in your life. They will show you who you currently are, and give you the opportunity to choose who you want to be. The mirror doesn't lie. What you see is what you get and what you are. But what you see does not have to remain the same. When you change the image in the mirror will too.

Remember and Forget!

In a strange way I guess I could say that my forefathers were teachers. They taught me everything that I did not want to be as a man. They never seem to grasp just how powerful their influence was as fathers. Each generation would remember the hurt, abuse, rejection and anger of the last one. Each generation made a promise to be better men than the last and each were unsuccessful. Like wounded soldiers, they all vowed in their hearts to remember what happened to them. Yet everyone of them failed to forget the lessons learned. That's where they went wrong! My forefathers never learned to remember and forget. In my own personal healing process I found that it was important for me to remember the things that happened to me and then to forget the lessons that I learned. So to this day I remember and honor the women and children in my family who were physically, mentally and verbally abused. But I choose to forget the ugly ungodly lesson that my fore fathers tried to teach or pass down to me. That is to use your power as a dad to beat your wife and children into submission. I became aware of one thing: a lesson learned is a lesson repeated. I was not going to repeat it.

When a father takes his son out to the back yard and teaches him how to catch a football, the father knows that the lesson is learned when his son catches the ball in the same fashion in which he did it. When a dad teaches his daughter how to shoot a basketball he knows that the lesson has been taught successfully when she begins to shoot the basketball just as he did. In the same way, when a father tells his child that he isn't good for anything he finds out that he has been successful when his child stares in a mirror one day and says to himself; "I am good for nothing." Like a complicated math problem he has finally come to the revelation of why two plus two equals four. The light has finally turned on. He finally learned what his father was trying to teach him. A lesson learned is a lesson repeated! They soon grow to be adults that find themselves saying to their own child the very thing that they promised they never would say; "You are good for nothing." Once again a lesson taught is a lesson repeated. That is until you learn to forget.

It is possible to remember what happened to you yet forget what you learned. For instance I remember struggling in a class my senior year in high school. It was clear that if I was going to improve my grade in the subject that I would need to get a tutor. The first day that I went to see the tutor I was taken by her beauty. Her champaign-colored eyes and delightful smile were enough to distract any high school boy. For weeks we would meet three days out of the week to study. By the time the test came I was sure that I was ready for it. I walked into the class room in all confidence and took my seat. Just then I remembered that I did not eat a good breakfast as my tutor taught me to do. I could feel my confidence began to shrink. The teacher gave us permission to start the test and when I turned the sheet over it was like I was reading Greek. Nothing made sense. Honestly all the test reminded me of was my tutor. Instead of doing my test I spent the next hour thinking of how I could ask her to be my girlfriend. In between creative ideas I answered a few questions. It seemed within a few minutes the teacher was telling us to put our pens down and we were passing our test forward to be corrected. Days later we received our test scores and I found out that I had received a very poor score. It was obvious that somehow I had forgotten what I learned. I was not able to repeat what I was taught. Looking back I can remember what happened to bring me and that wonderful tutor together but to this day I have forgotten what I learned. My test score proved that a lesson taught is not a lesson learned until it is a lesson repeated. On the good side, that beautiful tutor eventually became my wife. The bad news was she would soon find out what other lessons I had learned.

I would like to say that I was totally healed of all the rejection, abandonment, hurt and anger in my life before I got married but I can't. Even though I loved God and my wife, I still had issues. There were parts of me that were healing but the parts of me that were not healed were causing damage to my marriage. I loved my wife dearly but I was not always sure of how to communicate that love for her. It was clear that I had learned some lessons from my father because I was repeating some of his actions. You may say; "Brian how is it possible that your dad was not around and yet you learned some type of important life lesson from him that would effect who you would turn out to be as a man, husband and or father? I mean after all he couldn't say anything harmful to you if he was not there!" And I would say; "My father's absence spoke louder than any audible voice I had ever heard in my life." It was as if I had been mentored by abandonment and rejection. As time went on I realized it became more and more essential for me to remember what happened to me and forget the lessons learned. Because I now, too, was a husband and father, this now made me a teacher, a mentor. The bottom line is we father the way we were fathered. We mentor the way we were mentored. We love the way we were loved. We lead the way were led. We influence the way that we were influenced and we teach what we learned until we decide to come before God and say; "Lord teach me a better way!" That's just what I did. And I learned that my past does not determine my future!

CHAPTER 4

THE POWER OF BEING ABSENT

Who's Your Daddy
A GENERATION WHO DOESN'T KNOW ITS FATHERS

During my travels I have met many young people who do not know their fathers. Sometimes that means that he is not physically there other times this means he is mentally or emotionally not there. This becomes apparent while I'm giving my presentations. I follow my usual format by introducing myself and cracking some jokes to loosen up the crowd. Then I give the title of my speech: **Fatherlessness**. Without fail there are always those kids in the crowd who nonverbally say to me that they have a father at home. They have been living with him for the past sixteen years and are sure that they know him. Then, I either pass out a questionnaire and/or ask the crowd questions from it. The questions are only to set them up so that I can drive my point home. Usually, the majority of the audience is left stunned.

Here is a sample of those questions:
Questionnaire #1
What is your dad's favorite color?
What is one of your dad's favorite foods?
What does he like to do for fun and relaxation?

What is one of your dad's greatest accomplishments or moments as a kid?

What is one of your dad's greatest disappointments or moments as a kid?

What would your dad say was one of the most memorable moments he had with his own father? Good and then bad.

What is one of the most hurtful things anyone has ever said or done to him?

What is one of the most encouraging things anyone has ever said or done to him?

What is one of your dad's greatest accomplishments as an adult?

What would your dad say was the best and worst thing you ever said to him?

What would your dad say was one of the best moments he had with you?

What would your dad say was one of the worst moments he had with you?

What would your dad say was one of the funniest moments he had with you?

Why are they so shocked? They realize that they can't answer most of these questions. For most of them, their relationships with their fathers are distant and superficial. They do not know how to connect with their dads, and their fathers do not know how to connect with them. The lack of knowledge of these teens brought an awareness of a large relationship gap. This brought a sense of insecurity to those who lived with their dads and for the teens who did not know his/her father, a great desire to know a father or father figure like this.

Who's your daddy? This is a statement that has been used humorously for years in our society. Strangely, the laughing stops when one can not sincerely and confidently answer this question. Sorry to say, that is where many teens find themselves. What most young people find out is that their inability to answer this one question only leads them to other questions that they are unable to answer as well.

Identity

It's amazing how not being able to answer a question such as, "Who's your daddy?" can lead to a life time of struggling with one's identity. You never seem to be able to answer personal questions such as: Who am I? What am I? Why do I? Where am I? When do I? And finally, How do I? These all seem like rather simple questions, but that greatly depends on what the question pertains to. For example if I asked, "Who am I going to the dance with next Friday?" That's not that important in the grand scheme of things. On the other hand if I ask, "Who am I?" as a person. That may be a little more difficult for me to figure out. Especially if you are growing up in a world where the media tries to answer that question for you. If I ask myself, "Why do I write with my left hand instead of my right hand? That may seem irrelevant. But if I ask, "Why do I get so angry that I want to hurt people?" Now this becomes a very relevant question that must be answered. Because if left unanswered I may turn into a young man who grows up, can't control my anger and do physical damage to my family because I never could answer that one question. "Why do I?" It's when we can not answer these important, relevant questions of who, what, why, where, when and how that life becomes scary.

I remember as a young boy growing up asking myself all of these questions and never having an answer. One thing is for sure, it is difficult to find out who you are if you don't know whose you are. I can recall having friends who had active fathers in their lives. They didn't seem to have the world figured out, but I noticed there was a greater sense of identity there. After spending some time with some of these friends and their fathers, I realized that their dads had answered some of the questions pertaining to their identity. They either knew who, why, where when, or how, more than I did. Their fathers were mentors. They had traveled the road before them and could speak wisdom into their life, calm their fears and keep them focused. These men were playing a role in helping to shape and develop the identity of their children. Through their actions, they were saying you are loved. You belong to me, and this is who you are.

This is the model God himself left for us in scriptures when it came to father-children relationships. In the bible, Matthew 3:16-17, God gives mankind an example of just how important identity is. Here is Jesus, the son of God, about to have his right of passage ceremony, so to speak, and be baptized in front of friends, family and strangers alike. His cousin a well known preacher in his own right, John the Baptist, baptizes him by lowering him under water. As Jesus returns to the surface something incredible happens. The bible says that the heavens were opened and a voice from heaven said, "This is my son whom I love; with him I am well pleased." What was God doing? He grabbed the attention of creation and before Jesus' friends, family and future followers he spoke identity over his son. He said I love you son. You belong to me and I am proud of you. He said let me tell you whose you are so that you will know who you are. The statement that God spoke over his son contains the building blocks for every father to speak and release identity over his child. The statement consisted of

Acceptance: This is my son.
Affection: Whom I love.
Affirmation: With him I am well pleased.

This is still the blueprint for releasing identity. The ultimate Father, who is God, left the rest of us fathers a set of instructions on how to give our children identity.

Strangely enough after this monumental event, Christ was then sent into the desert to be tempted by the devil for forty days and nights. The bible records this in Matthew 4:1-11 that Satan himself tempted Christ in every way yet without prevail. During the temptation Satan consistently used the following statement to get the Son of God to betray all that his father had taught him, "If you are the Son of God, then..." With every tempting question and challenge Jesus would quickly reply back to Satan by using this statement,

"It is written...." Finally this passage of scripture ends by Christ commanding Satan to leave him and he states one more time, "For it is written!" Realizing that he can not win and in obedience to Jesus' command, the devil leaves his presence.

Call me crazy, but I don't think that it was a coincidence that immediately after God spoke identity over his Son that Satan came to test the strength of what was spoken. With every, IF YOU ARE THE SON OF GOD; he tested the very core of who Christ was and who His Father said He was. Satan challenged Jesus' identity. The devil knew that all he had to do in order to disrupt the eternal plan of God, which was to bring salvation to the world through His Son, was to get Christ to question his identity. Who are you? What are you? Why are you? When will you? Where will you? Finally, how will you? These are all questions that build and shape our identity and give us purpose. The man in every child's life should be there to help answer these questions.

The Devil knew that an insecure Messiah struggling with identity would wonder IF:

If his father loved him.

If he really was his father's Son.

If his father was proud of him.

If his father's word could be trusted.

If his father really had his best interest in mind.

IF, IF, IF, IF, IF, IF, IF! Satan knew that Jesus would not accomplish his mission if he was not sure of whose he was and who he was.

A savior with an identity crisis would have questioned his purpose and failed the world. With every identity crushing question and temptation, Jesus let it be known that he knew who, why, what, when, where and how. It was all summed up in this statement, "It is written!" What was he saying? "It is too late Satan. My Father has already spoken identity over my life." What Christ was really saying to Satan was MY DADDY SAID......

MY DADDY SAID HE loves me!

MY DADDY SAID HE is my Father!

MY DADDY SAID HE is proud of me!

MY DADDY SAID HE can be trusted!

MY DADDY SAID HE has my best interest in mind!

AND WHAT MY DADDY SAYS GOES! Jesus was saying, Satan you don't understand, when I say that it is written I don't mean on paper like the laws of the prophets or on stone like the ten commandments. When I say, "It is written!" I mean that it is written on my heart. It is written on the very core of who I am. It is my Identity. I come from good stock. I can not and I will not fail at what my father has sent me to do.

You see it was important the day that God grabbed creation's attention and announced that Jesus was His son whom He loved and was well pleased with. But for who? It was great that the family and friends of Christ was there to hear it. It was just as great that those who would soon become followers of Jesus were there to witness it. Most important was that Jesus not only heard it but received and believed it. For it would be him who would have to stand by himself later and face many tests and trials that only could be passed by a young man who had a healthy identity. We learn from this that it's important to tell others how much we love our kids but more important to tell our children. Because in the end the test will be theirs alone. It would not matter if anyone else changed their mind about who Jesus was and they did. All that would matter is that he didn't forget who he was.

As a young boy I was like many other teens. I lacked identity. Like Christ, many young people are being immersed in monumental events in their lives only to come back to the surface and not have a father speak any identity over their lives. There is no familiar voice stating to the nations that this is my child who I love and am well pleased with. There is only SILENCE. However, it speaks loudly. The silence greets them as a father and begins to shape and form their identity. They leave that event in their life only to also face the desert of life immediately just as Christ did. They are being tempted daily by the crazy things of this world. Life's circumstances are questioning them as if they are on trial for some heinous crime. Who? What? Why? Where? When? How? Every test demanding answers. Yet they have none. They have nothing to combat the IF's of life. They have no, "It is written's!" They have no, "My daddy said!" They are only left with IF:

IF I sleep with him maybe he will love me.

IF I he hits me it only means he really loves me.

IF I drink more alcohol maybe my inner pain will go away.

IF I do drugs with them maybe they will accept me.

IF I commit suicide will anybody care?

IF I were different would my father love me unconditionally? "IF!" It's a two letter word that haunts the soul of most teenagers in our country today.

What Does Your Absence Mean
Bad Decisions

It wasn't that I didn't know any better but, while in middle school I was making some very bad decisions. I started hanging out with one of the local drug dealers who went by the name of Big "C". Big "C" was about twenty years old, dressed sharp, drove nice cars, and had more money and jewelry than anyone I had ever known. Looking back, I think that the thing that drew me to him was that he accepted me at a time when everyone else thought that I was stupid. Big "C" drove me around in his nice cars and slipped me money all the time. He made sure that I had nice clothes and jewelry as well. He made me feel cool, especially when he would pick me up from school. All the kids would stand in awe of his Cadillac and loud music. The car would roll up with its gold rims and music so loud you could always hear him coming from blocks away. When the kids saw me with Big "C", I no longer felt stupid — I felt cool.

It took some time for me to realize that Big "C" was leading me down the wrong path of life. He had been an outstanding high school football player from the southern states. He was big, fast and strong and fatherless just like me. Even at the age of twenty and not having played football in years, Big "C" was still built like a truck. The truth was, even though it looked like he was cool, he wasn't. He was just hurting. Big "C" never went on to college and he didn't have a job, not a real job anyway. The worst part was that he was destroying his community with drugs. That was definitely not cool. Before long, his luck ran out and he became a part of the 75% of prisoners who grew up fatherless. He started dealing drugs because he was left to define what a man was for himself.

One day while making a drug deal, Big "C" got caught. I was thankful that I wasn't with him. Actually it was a miracle that I wasn't, because we were together every other day that week! When the cops arrested him, Big "C" had so many illegal things in his possession that he spent the next nine years in jail. After Big "C" went to jail, I went back to being plain old Brian. That was all right with me, because after seeing what happened to the "cool" drug dealers, one thing was for sure, I never wanted to end up behind bars. Looking back now I can see how my longing for the acceptance of a father led me into making a lot of bad decisions. Watch the media. Read the newspaper. Watch the youth around you. You will see that most of their bad decisions come from their longing to be loved by a father.

Sexual Activity

Is it possible for you to be a strong loving father who is involved in your kid's life and yet they make some bad choices in regard to sex? The answer is yes. However, reality is the chance of your child being sexually active greatly increases in your absence physically or verbally.

As men, how many times have we seen or heard some young man in a locker room discussing what he did to or with some girl over the weekend? Moreover, how many times was that young man us? Remember the stories about how we conquered every defense of some young lady? What about how we had so much charm that she just couldn't resist herself and had to give herself sexually to us.

I have long regretted my own youthful sexual escapades. I don't remember everything, but what I can remember is a young man who was searching for identity. And, everyday I was being told by the media that my manhood would be found in having sex. There was no father around to tell me differently. So, like a right of passage ceremony, I engaged in sex thinking that I would surely be a man after this. Immediately afterwards I would always feel some sense of false security in my manhood. I mean after all, I did go through the steps of what it takes to be a man right? Wrong! I found out that by the next day I would find myself still struggling with my self esteem as well as my identity. Who was I? What was I? Why was I still hurting inside? Nothing had changed, I was still a hurt, rejected child trying to find his way in life and looking for the love of a father.

What I came to realize was that the young women that I was sexually active with were also struggling to define themselves. Truthfully, had there been a healthy relationship with a male figure in any of their lives, there would have been less of a chance of me sleeping with them. Their fathers were either totally absent or there but not there. One thing was for sure, the kind words that I shared with them were not words that they were hearing from what should have been the real man of their lives, their fathers. When a young man tells a young girl how good she looks and she gets too excited about it, that is a great sign that her father doesn't affirm her very often. If a father does not discover and speak the love language of his child, some young man will. And believe me, she will respond. Studies show that adolescent females between the ages of 15 and 19 years of age, reared in homes without fathers, are significantly more likely to engage in premarital sex than adolescent females reared in homes with both a mother and a father.

I have dated girls who have had great to decent fathers as well. And never did I get involved with them sexually. There always seemed to be some need within them that already had been met. The nice things that you said and did for them were never something that they hadn't heard or seen before. But where had they heard it? Where had they seen it? Who was feeling this need? Who told them that they didn't need young men like us to make them feel like a woman? Who was speaking into their lives? There dads that's who. It was the power of dad. Their father's influence was greater than the media that said everybody's doing it. It was more powerful than affectionate words that were spoken by strangers passing in the night. The only time you heard these girls' names in the locker room was when guys were letting you know that you didn't have a shot in the world.

The same was true of my male friends who had great or decent fathers in their lives. They knew how to treat a young lady. They had watched the example of their fathers. They knew who they were as young men and had a game plan on waiting until they got married before they had sex. They understood that having sex did not constitute becoming a man. They were not swayed by the smooth talk of girls who wanted to be their first. As strange as that may sound those girls do exist. They constantly are chasing after men to fulfill a need that their father should have filled. They want to hear some one tell them they're pretty, they're the best, they're the only one, and that they are special. They want to hear someone say that you are my baby girl. Our presence as fathers to our children gives them permission to make a choice to be different. A choice and a chance to wait to give themselves sexually only after marriage vows have been taken.

Anger, Rejection, Abandonment

His parents had been separated before he was even born. Bill was now a raging mad teenager who had run his mother out of his life and had never seen his father before. He knew a few things about him. He knew his name, what he looked liked from pictures, that he was an angry, abusive man that he had rejected and abandoned him. Bill knew that his father was serving time in Jackson Prison for committing murder.

Moved with compassion for this young man's situation, Bill's grandparents took him in to raise him. Aged in years, yet with a lot of love to give, they figured they would need help in keeping their grandson on track. They introduced him to the local youth group connected with the church that they attended. They thought it would be helpful to get Bill around a group of positive teens and some great adult role models.

The youth Pastor still remembers the first day that Bill came to the youth ministry. He described him as cold, yet wanting. As time went on, the youth Pastor got to know Bill, through spending quality time with him he found out exactly what he was wanting. Bill was longing for a sincere relationship with a male figure. The only problem was that the hatred he felt towards his father never allowed him to open up and trust men in that way. He always wanted to ask his father "why did you leave me?" Not why you left my mom, but me. Whether you were with her or not, I still needed you in my life. One side of Bill wanted his father's love; the other side hated him. Bill hated his father so much that he vowed that he would never become like him. But what he didn't understand is that what we hate we tend to imitate.

One night after doing drugs and needing money to get more, Bill decided to rob the one place where he knew he could surely get the money, his grandparents' home. It happened over and over again in his life. Because he felt rejected, he rejected what seemed to be every good thing that came into his life. He loved others as he loved himself, and that wasn't a good thing. That night Bill and his buddies waited until dark, wore masks and broke into his grandparents' home. Not taking many precautions as to how they would get in or what would happen if his family were to wake up, they recklessly destroyed the home and grabbed money. Just as they were about to leave, his grandparents came out of their bedroom thinking that maybe their grandson was up late and being very disrespectful. When Bill and his drug crazed friends realized that they were caught they panicked. They grabbed Bill's grandparents and beat them unmercifully. Bill and his friends left the two people that loved him more than anything in the world for dead that day.

Bill's grandparents lived through this horrible ordeal. For some time they could not figure out who would do such a thing to them. Then police discovered that this horrible crime was committed by their own grandson. Out of tough love for Bill, his grandparents filed charges against him. No longer separated from his dad, today Bill is in Jackson state prison five cells down from his father. He can now ask him all the questions that he wants. Here is a father who definitely knows what his absence means. An alarming 85% of youth in prisons grow up in a fatherless home. So take a look back.

The steps of your son or daughter may be following your footprints down that long, dark and broken road that you travel.

CHAPTER 5

THE POWER OF BEING THERE!

What Your Presence Means
Protection

I had just finished speaking before five hundred teenagers sharing challenges of growing up fatherless. I ended my speech by sharing with them my new found excitement of now getting to be the one thing that I never had, a dad. Tears were falling and heads were bowed in grief. I knew that what I did next would be crucial to the healing of these broken youth. My story had broken them and now they needed my arms to hold them. If any true healing was going to continue, they were going to need more than my words. They were going to need my presence.

Crying myself by now, I gently persuaded them to come to the front of the auditorium if they just needed a shoulder to cry on. Being a former All-American football player, I'm a pretty good size guy with broad shoulders. But, even I could not bear the weight of the tears from the three hundred teenagers who came to the front. No linebacker or defensive lineman has ever hit me as hard as those teens' grief.

Realizing that the need was much greater than the supply, I asked the other leaders in the room to join me in ministering to the kids. We each grabbed as many hurting youth as we possibly could and we cried and prayed with them. When appropriate, we held them in our arms. No, we were not their fathers, but we gave them the presence of a father.

It was difficult to move from one distraught teen to the next, because some of them would put you in a bear hug and hold on for life. They weren't sure when they would feel the presence of a male figure who sincerely cared for them again. It was clear that they felt safe. It was as if life had become a continuous rain storm, and they had weathered it without shelter. That night, it wasn't that the rain stopped, the weather didn't matter much because they had protection. We were like much needed umbrellas making it possible for them to stay dry and brave the elements. That's how it is. Some teens have umbrellas and some don't. Some have fathers and some don't. Some have protection and some don't. Your presence means shelter.

Stability

That night two particular young women's stories stuck out to me. As much as they would say that I blessed them, I am sure that they blessed me even more. Through what they shared with me, I learned a little bit more of what a father's presence means.

The first young lady who came up to me was wiping tears from her eyes. However, she had the biggest smile on her face. She walked up to me and said, "Brian, I want to let you know that unlike most of the kids at this altar tonight I have a wonderful father. I listened to how much you loved your daughter and it reminded me of the love that my father has shown to me for eighteen years. He has always told me that he loved me even at my most embarrassing moments. He has even gone as far as to sing songs out loud to me in public declaring his fatherly love for me." Tears once again began to fall from her eyes. It was clear that she could hardly wait to get home and see her papa to say thanks. She went on to say, "Even the times that I acted like I didn't want him to do those things, it was what my heart longed for." Then she challenged me by saying, "Never stop loving or telling your daughter that you love her."

The young lady reached out to politely shake my hand and then began to walk away. Just as her hand was leaving mine I quickly closed the grasp of my hand to pull her back. Her head quickly turned to see why I was preventing her from leaving. I was stopping her from departing because I realized that this was a great opportunity for me to learn something I had never experienced before. Not to mention she had made statements about her father that I wanted my daughter to say about me someday. I asked her "Why was it so important that her father loved her that way? And, what did it mean to or do for her as a person?" She looked at me and without a second of hesitation she replied, "Mr. Pruitt, I have been a lot of places and met a lot of people, and not all of them have accepted, liked, or even loved me. But one thing that I have always known for sure is that at the end of the day I could always go home, and my dad would accept, like and love me." It was clear that for this young lady that was all that mattered to her. The love of her father left her with an immeasurable sense of stability.

Blessing B-Joy & Des

Brianna and Destiny are my two little angels. My blessings from God. They remind me that the favor of God is on my life. B-Joy and Des, that's what I call them. They are my baby girls, my opportunity to be a hero. Besides my wife and mother, I love no one on this earth more than these precious little girls. They have allowed me to love in ways that I never thought possible. In B-Joy and Des I see the purest form of innocence. I see what I was and what I long to once again be. Care free, trusting, forgiving, accepting of my self, bold, courageous and fearless. It seems as if they already know that there is no one like them on the face of the earth and that allows them to be okay with just being themselves.

I love those mornings when I awake to the beautiful sound of my little girls' soft unmistakable voices piercing the walls of the entire upstairs and knocking on the door of my heart. I roll out of bed and head to their bedroom, the muffled words to the songs that they are singing become clearer. Finally I get to their room and open the door. Childishly pretending as if they do not know that I have entered the room, they continue to sing one of their favorite songs. This song has comforted many generations of people throughout history. Yes! You guessed it. "Yes, Jesus loves me!"

I call their names. They peek their curly heads up. Their champaign colored eyes dazzles the room like the most beautiful sunrise. And like a Jack in the box, they spring to their feet and yell my most cherished words in the world, "Daddy, Pappa!" I stretch my arms out to pick them up. As I lift them, I ask, "How can two little girls with very few teeth make such wonderful smiles?" We walk over to their closets and pick out clothing that they will be wearing for the day. Then, they prepare for a very important moment that we have had every day of their lives. It's time for Daddy to speak a blessing over B-Joy and Des. I look into two sets of curious little eyes, and I began to say the following:

"No weapon formed against you shall prosper. Goodness and mercy shall follow you all the days of your life. You have the favor of God and the blessing of your father. Your Daddy loves you and he promises you that you will be blessed. You are blessed because your father says so and you are a friend of God."

This is the way that it has been everyday without fail since they were born.

And it is the way it will be for the rest of my life. This is important because it speaks value into the heart of a child. Your child knows that even if others are critical and unappreciative of their unique qualities, he/she is of great wealth to their dad. It says, "I am valuable, priceless in the eyes of my leader." I not only take the time to tell my children how I feel about them, but I also tell them how God feels about them as well. I let them know that because of Him and His mercy that they can expect good out of life. Your Daddy is here. Your God is here. Together we can face whatever comes our way.

Importance for Boys
Who will they be?

I was twenty seven years old and had been married for five years. I was about to have one of the most defining moments of my life. At the time, I was working at a church full time as a Youth Pastor. For two years I had been trying to get my Senior Pastor and one of my mentors, Brian Molitor, together to just talk about ministry and things that we were experiencing as a church. Little did I know that Brian and my Senior Pastor had already been talking for a while and had been making plans for renovating me and not our church.

As my Pastor and I took the two-hour drive to Midland, Michigan, we talked about sports and had a great time. Finally we pulled into Brian's driveway and there were ten other cars already parked there. I noticed some of the cars. I thought that maybe Brian, as usual, had a group of guys at his house planning on how they could impact the world. It was not uncommon to go to Brian's and meet people from all over the world at any given time. So I just assumed some big business meeting was taking place.

My Pastor and I got out of the car and made our way up the driveway. As we entered the house, there was Brian waiting to give me the biggest hug. As always, he looked down from his six-foot-three frame, opened his arms, and said, "My son." (Sometimes he calls me Pru, short for Pruitt). Not being so tall, my face went right into his chest and he gave me a firm squeeze. And it never fails whatever seems to be troubling me at that time in life no longer exists. I feel protected. I feel as if I can be myself. I feel accepted. I feel as if I am one of his biological children. I feel "Good."

As I slowly made my way into the living room area, I began to notice some very familiar faces. Sitting in a circle were several men who, at some point in time of my life, had played some significant role. Right in the middle of the room was an empty chair. In unison they looked at me and yelled surprise! I was still somewhat confused. I hated to disappoint them, but I let them know that it was not my birthday. It was obvious that they were celebrating something.

I wondered why these important men were gathered together for the first time in one place. Just then I felt a large familiar hand on my shoulder. It was Brian. He said, "Son, I know it's not your birthday, nonetheless we have come to this place today to celebrate you and who you are." He then directed me to have a seat in the empty chair that was sitting in the middle of the room.

I was still very much perplexed by the situation. What did he mean celebrate me and who I was? Brian went on to say, "I know that you have never had a dad to cover you, lead you or teach you what it means to become a man. We have all played some major role in your life and we want to bless you today. Though we are not responsible for who you are, we, as a collective group of men, want you to know that we will be responsible for who you will be. We will be a father to the fatherless. We will cover you, lead you and teach you to the best of our ability as to what it means to be a man."

By now tears were filling my eyes. I was in total shock. I could not believe that these men found me to be worthy to put their busy worlds on hold and come together to honor me. At that point for twenty seven years not even my own biological father had ever thought that I was worthy of his time. It seemed as if he didn't care about who I was and wasn't interested in who I would be. Yet these men saw something valuable in me when I didn't even see much value in myself.

Suddenly through the tears that were in my eyes, I could see blurred objects moving my way. All the men in the room began to bring gifts to me and sat them at my feet. These were not store-bought gifts. They were things that these men had kept in their possession for years. Some had received these items from very significant people in their own lives. They were all giving me something that had great value to them. As each one brought up their gift and handed it to me they would read a letter they had written to me. These letters were one to three pages long. In each letter they told me how they felt about me as a young man. They told me of the positive character traits and strengths that they had observed in me. They described and affirmed my God-given gifts and talents, and how they believed that those talents could be used to touch the world.

By now I was an emotional mess. I just sat there in total awe that this was happening to me. Just when I thought it was over, something else began to take place. These men brought their children with them. And each of them also came to me and handed me gifts that they cherished greatly. At first it felt strange taking a gift from a young kid, but these kids sincerely took the time to pick out just the right thing to express their love for me. Their unselfish acts melted my heart. With every gift given, like their fathers, they began to tell me their opinion of me. Most of them were younger than me. It was very clear that they held me in high esteem and wanted to thank me for my example of character and integrity.

When the last child finished sharing his thoughts, every man and child in the room was crying and then they slowly converged around me. There was a three-hundred-and-sixty-degree circle of loving fathers and grateful sons surrounding me. I felt safe and invincible. They began to pray aloud for me. They prayed for who I was as a young man and who I would be as a man, husband, and future father. With every word spoken, I felt renewed. Every word was being soundly placed to fortify my identity. I personally could now say for the first time in my life as Jesus did, "It is written!" or shall I say, "My daddy said!" to all the tests and trials of life. Someone had celebrated me! Someone had finally said, "This is my son who I am well pleased with." Someone had finally told me who I was. I am Brian Pruitt, a man of God, Character, Destiny, Purpose, Integrity, Conviction, Faith, Fire and Hope. Brian Pruitt is a warrior, always giving glory to God, at peace with himself, sure and sound in his decision making and yet not afraid to make a mistake, great husband and dad. I know who I am because my Fathers (mentors) told me so. They spoke into and over my life. They gave my journey a direction. They said, "Go west young man!" "There is a whole world out there waiting for you." The exciting part is that I had never been more sure of who I was and who I would be. I had a "look out world here I come attitude!"

<u>Importance for Girls</u>
<u>Who will they marry?</u>

Fathers play an important role in a young girl's life. From birth, his actions model the behaviors his daughter should expect in future relationships. If she grows up watching you be verbally or physically abusive, irresponsible, preoccupied, impatient, unfaithful, angry, uninterested, disrespectful, and driven, then don't be surprised when she chooses someone like that. If she watches you become a great father, husband, and man then she will expect her significant other to strive for greatness. In most cases, you are the prototype.

I am a young father. However, I think about my daughters' future husbands. Will they love them the way that I do? Will they make them laugh like me? Will they speak a blessing over their life the way I have done for years? Will their husbands speak that same blessing even when she is unkind? Will they love my girls for better or worse? Will they love B-Joy and Des until death does its part? I know that it seems ridiculous to ask yourself these questions when your children are still young. But these are the things that all loving fathers want to know.

Reality is that your daughter sees her future husband in you. When you come from a dysfunctional home, dysfunctional becomes the norm. Your daughter will find someone to maintain her norm. For example, she may leave a bad relationship only to later return or get involved in a relationship that is similar to the one she just left. You set a standard and there is a great chance that she won't exceed it. During a time of introspection, ask yourself if you're the person you want your daughter to marry?

In recent years I have learned that not only do my actions towards my daughters teach them what to expect from men but also my actions toward their mother. The wild thing that crossed my mind during this time was that my wife's father probably shared my same fears regarding me. He probably thought to himself: Would he love her the way that I do? Would he speak a blessing over her life even when she seems to be unkind? Would he love her for better or worse? Will he love her until death does them part? My wife is somebody's daughter. And, he loves her just as much as I love my daughters. He wants the best for his child, just as much as I want the best for my children.

My daughters have made me look at my wife in a whole new way. Not as a child, but as someone's little beauty who has placed a great responsibility on me of loving her as much or more than they do. To live up to the standard that has been set for her is a great challenge considering the great father she has. My father-in-law is a model husband and father. My wife expects nothing less because of the standard her father set. As the first male figure in her life, he has really put the pressure on me. Likewise, I plan on leaving that pressure for the young men who will marry my daughters. Be the man today that you want your daughter to marry tomorrow.

CHAPTER 6

THE POWER OF COMMUNICATION AND APOLOGIES!

We Are The Youth Of The Nation!

They are the youth of the nation and they are hurting. Yet, very few people are asking them why. This section of the book has been dedicated to giving the youth a voice. You will hear about their successes and failures. We are allowing them to tell us about the influence that their fathers have had on their lives. Some stories are heart breaking enough to make you cry, while others are awesome enough to make you smile. My hope is that as you read each letter you clearly see the power of dad.

Dear Dad,

I can remember staying up late and waiting for you to come home. I always wanted to be around you, I would call everything and everyone Wes. But one day that all changed you were gone and I felt abandoned and confused. Growing up and not knowing if I was ever going to see you again tore me up inside. I can remember visiting you in jail and wondering why I was even going to see you. Eventually the visits stopped and I felt as though part of me was missing. Whenever I would see a daughter and a dad together I would wonder what it would be like to have you around. It brought more confusion and hurt than you could ever know. I wish that I could say that the confusion and pain are gone, but I can't. The more I know that you are part of me it makes me angry with you because of the poor choices you made have drastically affected my life. While you are the one that is in prison, I feel that I am in prison right there with you because I have built up walls and will not let anyone get close because I am afraid that they will hurt me as much as you have. I often second-guess people because you have taught me to not trust. While you may not have said it to me, you have shown me through your actions or rather lack of actions. Even now, I am afraid that I will marry someone just like you and they will end up leaving me. Your choices have caused me to hate myself because I don't even feel like I know who I really am. I feel like I am being pushed towards other people to find the fatherly love that I never felt from you. I have cried for you more than I even cry for myself. You are supposed to be my hero, protector, encourager, cheerleader, refuge and friend, but instead you are a poor role model, discourager, and coward. You have failed me as my father and somehow I feel as if it was my or my mother's fault, but now I have come to realize that the only one to blame is you. You are the cause of most of my pain and shame. I feel like I have to hide you from others because if they find out my dad's in prison for life they will reject me as I have even rejected myself. I was ashamed to tell others about you because I thought they might only care for me because they felt sorry for me rather than because of who I really am. I can only wonder if you knew how much your decisions were going to affect me. I would hope that you would. Due to my relationship with God, I have received the fatherly love that I didn't receive from you and I have learned to forgive and to love you. Through all of this, I still love you and I do want you to be a part of my life.

Sincerely,
Kesha

Dear Daddy,

From the very beginning you were always there for me. I can remember when I was little and if I ever had an injury you would tell me, "It's okay pumpkin I am here." I know that regardless of what happens in my life you will always be there to celebrate in my happiness, to wipe away my tears when I am sad, to encourage when I am disheartened, and to correct when I am wrong. When I was in high school, I can remember becoming so frustrated that I would begin to cry and you would put your arm around me and go over the homework again and again until I finally understood it.

When I was playing sports, you were one of my biggest fans regardless of how many times I swung and missed the ball or how many times I missed a free throw you would be in the stands telling me that I would get it the next time. You taught me that I could succeed in anything if I only put my heart into it. Not only are you protector, encourager, and cheerleader, but you are also my teacher. Through the way you live your life I have learned the importance of integrity. You have taught me to let my yes be yes and my no be no. While you never demanded perfection, you did demand honesty. You truly taught me that a man is always as good as a word. I can still hear you saying if someone will lie to your face, they will eventually be willing to do anything to you. I cannot remember one time over the course of my life in which you have broken your word to me or to anyone else.

I remember before I started dating you took me out on a date to show me how I was supposed to be treated. What you didn't know Dad is that I already knew how I was supposed to be treated because you demonstrated it to me every day of my life. You treated me as a princess and always told me to settle only for a prince. The most valuable lesson I have learned from you is to truly love and trust God. You have always taught me that God is to be first in my life and if I am striving to please Him everything will work out. Having you as a father has made it so easy to love and trust my heavenly father because you have been the perfect model of what a dad is suppose to be. If I didn't have you as my dad I do not believe that it would be as easy for me to trust God because earthly fathers are here to demonstrate what our heavenly father is like. The second most valuable lesson I have learned from you is how to really treat and love people. You have always emphasized the importance of looking for the best in people and to take the time to really listen to people. Whenever I was having a problem with someone and they didn't apologize, you would tell me to forgive them and to continue to love them regardless of what they had done.

Dad you have always taught me that heroes are the people who step out of the crowd and do what everyone else should be doing. I just want you to know that you are my hero and I love you with all of my heart. Thank you for teaching me to love God, to love people and to never give up. You have impacted my life and have helped to mold me into the person that I am today. While it isn't much the only words I can say are thank you!!!

Love Always, Michelle

Dear Dad,

Everyone use to tell me that I was too mean and shy. I never understood why they said that about me. Yeah, I had my little issues with not opening up to people and I felt insecure. I use to consider myself as an odd teenager. Everyone told me that I was very beautiful and intelligent but I never thought that those statements were true. I never trusted anyone because I thought that they were going to stab me in the back and smile in my face.

From my point of view I was always known as the lame, the quiet one, fearful, the mean one and least but not least the reject. As a young child my mind often wondered why I would label myself those harsh titles. I was so determined to figure out what sparked this self hatred and the cold feeling of neglect.

I remember as a child experiencing the feelings of rejection when I asked my mom, "Why my dad never came to see me." She told me, "you had made a bad mistake and we had to leave you." Ever since that day I noticed myself having daily issues of hating people for no reason, feeling depression. Having anxiety attacks from being around people. Feeling rejected and hating all males as if they were the person who hurt me.

The last time I talked to you on the phone you seemed as if you were a little child yourself. I actually felt sorry for you because you seemed so lost. Ever since that day we have had an off and on again relationship. I feel so distant from you. We were like two confused children. You didn't know how to be my father and I didn't know how to be your daughter. I guess we both have learned to live in separate worlds.

Sincerley, Melissa

Dear Brian Pruitt,

When I was four years old my father left me. He was always drunk and that made him very mean. The last thing that I remember being four years old and being beat for asking him why he drank so much. He left my family the next day.

I was the youngest of four kids. My mom had to work real hard to take care of our family. She did a good job at keeping us in church. But with my father gone and mom working so hard I grew up missing a lot of love and attention. It left a really big hole in my life. My mom remarried to a very nice guy eventually. He tried to love me like a father but by then I was strung out on drugs and I was only nine years old. At the young age of fourteen I left home to find out what was missing in my life. This led me to a bad heroin addiction which led me to prison.

Sincerely, John

Dear Brian Pruitt,

My real dad has never been in my life. I use to see him when his sister would pick my brother and I up and take us to her house. But even then I only saw him a couple of times. He was always to busy doing drugs. He was addicted to cocaine. I remember it like yesterday he came to get me it was the only and the last time. I was going to spend the night at his house and on the way he made a stop at a friend's house. He left me in the car and walked over to this group of guys and had bought some coke. He came back to the car sniffing. Well, that was the last time I ever saw him.

Over the years my mom has had a few boyfriends a couple even lived with us.

I would get attached and they would just leave. Finally my mom got married to this one guy that I barely even knew. He verbally and physically abused me. Then he and my mom got a divorce. I was so happy but my mom was very sad. I felt bad for my mom. She then got another boy friend but they broke up. The good news was that I liked him and even though he was no longer with my mom he still let me come over his house and do my home work. I really loved him. Then something horrible happened. He was killed by his ex-girl friend. The night before he died he came over to say goodbye to me and my brother. It tore me from limb to limb to lose him.

As you can see I have not had very good luck with men in my life. They have either not been good to me or they have died.

Thanks, Jamie

Over the years I have held thousands of wounded teens in my arms. We have cried and laughed together. Often I will just let them talk and share their feelings with me. After they are done talking, I would apologize on behalf of all men that hurt them. I would look them straight in the eyes and I say, "I am sorry that I hurt you, let you down, disappointed you, missed your birthday, graduation, prom, sporting event, for what I said and didn't say, didn't take the time to do that, was not the man or dad that you needed."

The results are incredible. Often, healing begins to take place. All this time this wounded heart has been longing to hear someone say, "I'm sorry." Communication and apologies go a long way.

Fatherless or Childless: What's Worse?

As a child, teen and young adult like many of the fatherless youth of our country. It never crossed my mind that it just might be worse to be childless than fatherless. This question never came until I became a father. Seeing the birth of my two angels, changing pampers, watching them crawl for the first time, hearing their first words, watching them take their first step, teaching them their colors, alphabets or how to count to ten, ride their big wheel, wrestling with them in the yard under a summer sun, teaching them to swim, dancing with them in the living room, playing super hero's, teaching them to fish and camp, having them try to get an understating of the world by asking a thousand questions, you giving them an answer only to have them reply, "But why?" Leaving you to come up with another answer. How about doing something that they love so much that they say, "Do it again daddy!" "Do it again!" Or walking in the house after a long day's work and having them run screaming your name and jumping into your arms. Last but not least. Having their arms wrap around your neck and hear them say, "I love you daddy!"

Now that I have experienced all these things I am not so sure if it is worse to be fatherless or childless. The only thing that I can think of that would hurt me more or as much as growing up fatherless would be to miss out on all the joys that my children bring to me. When I say childless I am not referring to those that are unable to have children or that have lost a child to tragic circumstances out of their control. When I say Childless I am referring to men who have made a conscious choice not to be involved in their children's life. As well as those men who have been banned by the other parent from building a relationship with their child. They are childless. Meaning that they have the ability to enjoy the joys that a child can bring yet they have consciously chosen not to or they are being blocked from doing so. What a life. To look back and realize that you missed out or were denied one of the greatest joys in life, fatherhood.

I look at things in a whole new light as a father. As a young person I thought I would be one of the lucky ones if I had a father to hold me in the air after scoring a touchdown, or shouting my name in the crowd. But now I think just a little differently. Now I think I am one of the lucky ones because I am a father who gets to hold my children up after great accomplishments. I get to stand in the crowd with school colored t-shirts and their names in bold letters and root them on. I get to create our own little world in our back yard. For years my heart went out and my ministry was directed towards the fatherless. But once I became a dad and shared in those wonderful unspeakable moments, I realized not only all the things that I missed as a child that my children were getting to experience, but, all the things that my dad missed as a father. I felt and experienced joys that he would never know. That day my heart began to break for my father. I had already forgiven him many years ago. But then and only then did I feel compassion for him. During this time in my life through some strange turn of events my father and I talked by phone. I let my dad know that he had a wide open door to my home and my children. I wanted him to feel the joy of fatherhood. The conversation ended and I have still not seen my dad. He has chosen to remain childless.

I thank God that he has not only opened doors for me to go to the fatherless but also to the childless men and bring healing to this wound. Believe me these men are hurting. A census has been taken which tells us that 24 million and growing youth are father-less. But no one has ever done the research to tell us how many broken hearted childless fathers are out there. There are many men hurting for the love of a child, longing to say, "I'm sorry," or hurting because of regret. I'm sure many of these fathers wonder what it would be like if......

They dream of `themselves in the back yard in their own little world with their child. "One, forty two! Hut, hut, hut!" "Do it again daddy! Do it again!" Now you tell me is it worse to be fatherless or childless?

What God Has To Say

We have heard the voices of the youth of the nation. The question is what does God have to say about men and their relationship with their children? By no means has God been silent about this topic. Malachi 4:5-6 says, "See, I will send you the spirit (Heart) of Elijah ....He will turn the hearts of the fathers to the children and the hearts of the children to their fathers; or else I will come and strike the land with a curse." (NIV)

Another translation reads this way:
Malachi 4:6 "I will send Elijah....................He will convince parents to look after their children and children to look up to their parents. If they refuse, I'll come and put the land under a curse." (The Message)

Heart of Elijah & Hunger of Elisha

Who is Elijah? Elijah was an Old Testament prophet who had a compassionate heart for the generations coming behind him. He was a great role model and leader. He understood the importance of leaving a legacy. He understood that the life that you're living today is the legacy that you're leaving for tomorrow. Even though he had no known biological children he took a young man by the name of Elisha underneath his mentorship. For quite some time Elijah taught Elisha everything he knew. He taught him in word and deed. He allowed him to see what he was doing, do what he was doing and then challenged him to teach what he had been taught. As they went on their journey Elijah constantly challenged Elisha's commitment or desire to be mentored by giving him permission to leave his side as they entered each city. It never failed Elisha declined Elijah's offer knowing that there was so much more to learn. It was a wonderful relationship. Elisha respected Elijah and Elijah accepted Elisha. Finally the Mentor asked the Mentee," What can I give to you for your faithfulness?" The young man said "I would like to have double of your spirit, heart, anointing, talent, knowledge, wisdom."

This was something that only your first born biological child could or should ask for. However, to our knowledge Elijah did not have any biological children. So he agreed but only on one condition. The requirement would be that Elisha would have to follow him to the end. He would have to be by his side as he passed from this life to the next. Elijah told him "If you see me when I am taken from you it will be yours otherwise not." Elisha accepted the challenge as usual, thinking to himself I have come too far to turn back now.

The bible goes on to tell the story of how these two awesome individuals continued on their journey. One day as they were doing what they always did, that is, respecting and accepting one another, the scriptures say that they were walking and talking. Suddenly they were separated as Elijah was taken by a chariot of fire and entered into heaven. Elisha saw this and cried out "My father!" "My father!" Elisha was grief stricken. He had lost the man who believed in him, accepted him. The man that made him believe that there was no obstacle that he could not overcome. He would soon find out that he gained what he asked for, a double portion of his mentor's spirit, heart, talent, anointing as he was promised.

What can we learn from the heart of Elijah and the hunger of Elisha? We learn that every good mentor mentee relationship has someone who wants to be respected and someone who wants to be accepted. As an adult you probably desire respect from your children and your children desire to be accepted by you. If you can develop these two things in your relationship with your children then you have an atmosphere to build something wonderful.

Notice that the heart of Elijah was to pour into the next generation to leave a legacy. He could have taken his gifts, talents, wisdom and anointing with him to heaven, but he did not. Why? I believe that Elijah understood a couple of things. He understood that God did not need any miracles performed in heaven, no prophecies given in heaven, no wisdom given in heaven, no incredible talents displayed in heaven. So with that thought in mind Elijah said "Since there is no need for these things in heaven I should just leave them here on the earth. Not in an irresponsible way but responsibly. He left them with a young man who had proven to be faithful to the end. He left his gifts, heart, anointing and talents with Elisha. He left them on the earth because they could not be used in heaven.

Too often we have people who are talented, gifted, wise and anointed who take their gifts with them into the next life only to find out that they can't be used there. They are leaving this life with their hands full instead of empty. They mentor no one they leave nothing for no one. They take every ounce and every one of there talents with them.

I don't know about you but my desire is to pour into the next generation biological and non-biological children and leave a legacy. My hope is to do what Elijah did to leave this place with my hands and my heart empty. To find responsible young people to pour my heart, gifts, talents, anointing into so that when I am long gone my gift is still doing a work in the earth. That's what Elijah did. He was long gone but for years after his leaving the earth his heart was touching, healing, challenging, encouraging people through a young man named Elisha that he mentored. Question! How many generations will you still touch long after you are gone? Just because I have died does not mean my message or purpose or passion has. Let it live on. Give it away. Don't take it with you, leave it.

What did we see in each one of the written letters of the young people we read? We saw: The hunger of Elisha. A generation crying for acceptance. And, a generation willing to carry on a legacy if we will pass on or leave them with a well lit torch. We heard an army saying take the time to leave me with double and I will follow you to the end. A tender hearted warrior shouting, "My father!" My father!"

What is our Challenge or Mission as men or fathers of our nation? It is to, like Elijah, have a heart that says, "We will leave you better than we found you." Starting today we will leave you a legacy. We will leave you a well lit torch that shall be a lamp unto your feet and a light to your path. We love you and we are sorry that too often we have left this earth hands and heart full. We commit to taking the time to give our talents, gifts, wisdom, anointing and give it away. We will leave this life with heart and hands empty. We understand that God will not be running any business meetings in heaven so we will leave our knowledge on how to run a business with you. God will not need our athletic talents in any heavenly competitions so we will take the time to leave them with you. God will not be selling any real-estate in heaven so we will leave the knowledge on how to purchase it with you. God does not need web design or web sites in heaven so we will teach you. We will give it away! In full expectation that you too will grow up and find time to give what God has given you away.

The Turning (Burning for a Turning)

God continues to speak on the topic of fathers and their relationships with their children in the next verse. Letting us know that his heart is burning for a turning.

Malachi 4:6 He will turn the hearts of the fathers to the children and the hearts of the children to their fathers; or else I will come and strike the land with a curse. (NIV)

What does it mean to turn your heart? In the Old Testament the word turn simply meant: To turn back, carry again, go back home again, recover, refresh, rescue, restore and reward. God's heart is burning for this type of turning.

His name was Spencer. I met him at one of the many youth conferences that I speak at across the country but he represented so many teens I have had the opportunity to meet in my travels. Spencer sticks out in my mind because I remember running into this kid a few times that weekend. He seemed very closed to anything that I had to say, but I have seen this before as well. The one thing that I have learned is to always keep in mind that there is a story behind every face. People are the way they are for a reason. Life's victories, defeats, joys and pains like a well trained artist painting a fine piece of abstract art have shaped them into who they are. I wondered all weekend what was Spencer's story. The last night of the conference I found out. In ending my session I gave the young people a challenge. It became clear that Spencer wanted to take the challenge but he realized that he needed healing first. The teens who wanted to respond did so. I spent some time counseling and praying for young people afterwards. Just when I thought that I had finished talking with the last teen and was headed to relax, Spencer showed up. He no longer looked closed. He looked needy. He looked like he just needed someone to talk to. I walked up to him shook his hand introduced myself asked his name and asked him if there was anything he would like to talk about. Before he could get a word out of his mouth he started weeping. I held him in my arms we cried together.

At the time I was not sure what was wrong but it didn't matter to him or me. As he cried through clutched teeth and tried to fight back the waves of pain he said, "I'm so lonely!" At that moment it was like a dam broke. Each time he said it, "I'm so lonely!" The tears rushed and the emotions flowed. That night he told me how it was almost as if he was invisible to his dad. He said, "My dad is a great provider we have everything we need and want, everything but him." "I would trade everything he buys for me for just a little bit of his time." "I don't need material things I just need his attention. "I don't need his wallet I need his heart to turn towards me." "I'm so lonely.

Reverse The Curse

Malachi 4:6 ends by saying that if hearts are not turned the land will be cursed. The word cursed means: To be afflicted with harm. The last topic that God deals with in the Old Testament is that of father child relationships. Then he warns us that if we do not do well or have our hearts turned towards one another that we would bring or afflict harm on ourselves. What do I see in my travels? I see the curse. What do I hear in the voice of every wounded teenager's life? The curse. What do I see in every tear that falls from their face? I see the curse.

You might be saying at this time, "Brian, what in the world are you talking about? I don't believe in curses and I have not noticed that my kid or any other kid for that matter is under a curse." How would I reply to that statement? I would simply say remember the definition that I gave you of a curse first of all. Once again that is to afflict harm. I am not some space cadet who is curse crazy. I believe that the blessing of God is greater than any curse that I or anyone can afflict upon me. I am simply saying that a curse can be described as something as simple as afflicted pain. So let's make sure that we are using the same definition. Now with that thought in mind let me further explain. When a teen tells me that he is hurt or wounded from the relationship or lack of relationship with his father it says to me that we have inflicted pain on our own children. We have cursed them. When teens cry themselves to sleep at night wondering if we will notice that they even exist the next day, that tells me we have inflicted pain on our own children. We have cursed them. When I meet a young man whose last memory of his mother is watching her die at the hands of his father and now he is a young man full of anger, it tells me that someone has inflicted him with pain. Someone has cursed him. When I meet a young lady who tells me that her heart is being ripped in two right along with her parents marriage and that she is being forced to choose between the two people that she loves more than anything in the world, it says that someone has inflicted her with pain. Someone has cursed her. Do you get it? You say, "Get what?" The curse that we have self inflicted upon our children and ourselves is pain. The curse is pain. God was warning us in Malachi 4:6 to turn our hearts towards one another before we cause each other unbearable pain. Pain too much for any child to take and so great that it is even unbearable for a grown man.

The good news is as I said earlier that God's blessing is greater than any curse.

So as badly as we have wounded our children that's how much we can be a part of them being healed. The relationship can be restored. In God there is hope! This means that you can reverse the curse. The healing you can bring is much greater than the pain that you can inflict. Make up your mind that today will be the day that I began to reverse the curse. I will bring healing and not pain.

Saying I'm Sorry

If you were to write a letter of apology to your child what would it say? Remember that your child's perception is their reality. This means you may be apologizing for something you don't even believe or realize that you've done. But if your teen has made it known that you have hurt him or her in any way then it is their reality and it should be respected. We're not here to win an argument. We are here to win our child's heart. Win the war not the battle. Also keep in mind that it may take you one day or may be one month to finish your letter depending on who you are and the complexities of your relationship. Nevertheless, be committed to follow through with this. It may be the very thing that turns your child's heart towards you. Bottom line, if we are man enough to wound them let's be man enough to heal them.

The following exercise is designed to help bring healing to your child's heart by simply saying what you are sorry for. It is your chance to write the world's biggest apology to your child for things you have done that may have hurt them. Follow the statement, **"I am sorry for?"** By writing things that you want your child to know that you are sorry for. For example: I am sorry for being too busy for you at times. I am sorry for not attending events that were important to you. I am sorry for etc....

The next section of your letter is what **You hope for**. So you will follow the following statement, "I hope that?" For example, I hope that you will continue to invite me to your special events. I hope that we can start over etc....

Next your letter will move into one **special moment** that you and your child had together and describe that moment, how you felt and what you enjoyed about it. For example: I remember teaching you to ride your bike for the first time. I was blessed because you trusted that I would not let you fall. I was so proud when you finally made it down the driveway by yourself. It was one of the joys of my life.

Finally you will end your letter with the section that tells your child **what they mean to you**. For example: I want you to know that you mean the world to me. I want you to know how valuable you are to me.

Upon finishing this letter it is now up to you to make sure that you get it into your child's hands. If you live with your child, when you see them today hand it to them. If your child lives in another home, city, state or country get an address and mail it to them. You have nothing to lose and everything to gain.

The World's Biggest Apology

I'm Sorry For?

_____
_____
_____
_____

You Hope for?

_____
_____
_____
_____

One Special Moment:

_____
_____
_____
_____

What They Mean To You:

_____
_____
_____
_____

Signed _____

Dated_____

CHAPTER 7

Kryptonite and Superman

Turning The Tide

One of my favorite childhood super heroes was Superman. I remember a particular scene from one of the movies. The world was in trouble, and Lex Luther and his evil villains were causing total chaos. The world and everything in it was literally falling apart due to a man-made earth quake. It was a scene of massive destruction. Trees, homes, buildings, and people were being swallowed up by the earth while, Lex and his bandits stood in laughter. Meanwhile the love of Superman's life, Lois Lane, was driving her car in a frantic attempt to escape the coming judgment. Sadly to say, she too would be killed in the midst of the disaster.

Normally in a Superman movie, this would not be a problem. This would be just about the time that the "Man of Steel" would come flying out of nowhere to save the day. However, this time was different. Through much research Lex had found out how to stop Superman. He found his weakness, Kryptonite. It was a green glowing rock that could sap every ounce of Superman's strength from him. By some strange turn of events during the chaos, the Kryptonite was removed from Superman's presence, and he regains his strength. His super powers return. Immediately, he begins to try to save the world.

Lois Lane was the first person on top of his list to save. When he finds her, she is in dire straits. It's too late. The love of his life is dead. Totally distraught, in disbelief, and grieved would be the words that would best describe the look on the super hero's face. As tears run down his face, he holds Lois in his arms. Superman was out of his element he was too late. He had never been too late before. He had failed. He had never failed before. He lost a loved one due to his own weakness. If he only had gotten there in time. If he only had just a little more time. Time! That was it.

Superman's countenance suddenly changes as he wipes away his tears. He lays Lois down and stands to his feet as if he had a plan. With a shout, he raises one fist towards the sky and takes off flying through the air faster than light. He then began to circle the earth in a counterclockwise motion. Faster and faster and faster. As he did this every destructive, hurtful and evil thing that had been done on the earth was reversed and restored. Walls were replaced. Cars were sucked back up from the earth and cracks in the earth's foundation were shut. Buildings restored and people brought back to life. Order was restored. The process was so grueling that he burns himself out only to fall thousands of miles back to the earth which gave off the sound of an atomic bomb. He leaves a hole the size of the grand cannon. You are sure that he is dead at this point, but he is not. Sapped of his strength, dirty and worn he slowly rises to his feet and finds the ability to find the love of his life Lois Lane. When he finds her, this time, she is alive. Why? Because he has flown around the earth so fast that it has reversed time. The earthquake hasn't happened yet. He saves the world and the love of his life. Lex Luther and his bandits once again have been beaten. Superman wins again.

When all the odds were working against him, what did Superman do? He turned the tide. He literally turned back time and faced his greatest fear, the loss of Lois Lane. He was certain that if he did not do anything, he was going to lose the most important relationship in his life. He knew that he would have to fight to restore his relationship. So he faced his fear to gain his prize. What was his fear? Failure. What was the prize? A restored relationship with the love of his life.

Let me make this clear to you. You are Superman. Your child is Lois Lane, the love of your life. Due to circumstances in or out of your control the relationship has died. The walls have caved in on it. An earthquake of disagreements, obstacles, and fears has shaken your relationship to its foundations leaving a chasm too great to cross. The dreams of what you wished you had with your child have crumbled into pieces leaving only ashes. In the aftermath, your child is lost. Your greatest fear has come upon you. You're too late. You've failed. The relationship is dead. You stand there like Superman tears running from your eyes distraught about what you have lost. At this moment you can throw in the towel and feel sorry for yourself. The other alternative is to dig to the deepest part of you, face your fears, refuse to accept the relationship as it is, and muster up the strength to head towards the stars so that you can turn the tide.

I encourage you to take action! Turn the tide! If you do nothing you already know what the results will be. But if you face your fears, you just might be able to bring the relationship with your child back to life. I know that you can't reverse time but you can redeem it. Meaning that you should use it to your benefit from here on out. And if you can do that, you can turn the tide. Like Superman, you do everything in your power to right the wrongs. Apologize where and when needed. Ask for forgiveness when appropriate. Ask for permission to see that child again if you live separate from them. Make an effort to spend time with them if they live with you. Make a commitment that you are going to be consistent about rebuilding what has been torn down. Resolve in your heart that you won't quit until your relationship with your children has been restored. Remember that the relationship did not get like this overnight, and you may or may not be able to turn the tide overnight. Nevertheless, you can turn the tide. You must be diligent, consistent, and convinced.

You must face your fears. What fears? The fear of rejection, abandonment and failure. You say, "But, Brian what if I try to restore the relationship and my child rejects me?" "What if I wear my heart on my sleeve, stretch my hand out as a sign of peace, and my child abandons me or leaves me standing there alone?" "What if my child reminds me of my failures or begins to point out each one of my flaws while in an angry rage?" And I would say, "Whatever you fear is what your child feels." If you fear rejection your child is probably feeling rejected. If you fear abandonment then your child more than likely feels abandoned. Yet and still even knowing this we must be prepared to turn the tide. You turn the tide by facing your fears.

Childhood Dreams

Remember when you were a child waking up on Saturday morning to the fresh aroma of your mother cooking breakfast. You slowly roll over to be blinded by the sun that somehow sneaked its rays through your closed blinds. Startled by the glare you throw the pillow over your head. Peeking through one eye you look in the direction of your superhero alarm clock. Realizing that it's nine o'clock in the morning, you jump to your feet in full excitement. Frantically looking for the remote control, you toss everything in your room to the floor. "There it is!" As you hit the power button, you begin to feel your stress subside. Mom knocks on the door and hands you a plate of the world's best breakfast. Your favorite theme song starts playing. You work the rabbit ears on the antenna, and finally the picture comes in clear. There he is. Your favorite super hero, Batman, Superman, Flash, Green Lantern, Thunder cats, He-Man. This is the guy that you dressed up as every year at Halloween. This is the person that you have always dreamed of being. There he is in all his glory with muscles bulging, hair glowing, smile shinning and costume perfectly customized and fitted to the tee.

When you were a child that super hero represented everything that you wanted to be. When you saw him you did not see his face. You saw your own face with his body. You saw yourself saving the world, that child, that lady. You saw yourself lifting that car above your head, holding a twelve story building up with one hand and directing traffic with the other. And at the end of each day people would stand in the streets and applaud you for all that you had done. There was no way you were going to allow hurt or harm to come to the earth and or its inhabitants. You were a super hero.

We all have memories of childhood dreams rather that consist of being a super hero or the daunting task of being a better man than your father. For good reasons, four generations of children in my paternal family have tried to become better than the next. It's easy to want to be a better man than my absent and abusive father.

My goal was not only to be a better man than my father, but to be the super hero to my future family. The hope of every good or bad father is that their son or daughter will be better than them. You may think that to be strange. But you go to work everyday to give them the best of what they need, save money every check so that they can attend the best college, and get a life insurance policy that financially prepares them in your absence. Even if you are a good man and your child stands in awe of you, you still desire your child to have more, go further and be better. Of course this never means that you don't allow them to be themselves, but you want the best for them. You want them to avoid the mistakes that you made.

Your moment is here! It's your time and your turn. To make your childhood dream come true. That is to be a better man or as good of a man as your father.. Remember that you represent everything that your children either desire to be or not to be. When they see you they see their face on your heroic body and performing your feats of strength. When they see you they see themselves saving the world, that child, that lady. When they see you they see themselves lifting that car above their head, holding a twelve story building up with one hand and directing traffic with the other.

And at the end of each day they are the ones who stand in the streets of our lives and applaud us for all that we have done. They are the ones that will act as a mirror to let us know if we in fact have become better than or as good as our fathers. They will be the determining factor of whether our childhood dreams have or have not come true. If we have become better men they will look at us in awe and take refuge in the thought that there is no way we are going to allow hurt or harm to come to their world and its inhabitants. To your child you are Superman, You are a super hero.

Clark Kent VS. Superman

If I were to ask you who would win a battle between Clark Kent and Superman, without blinking an eye, you would say of course Superman. After all, Superman is practically unstoppable. He has unspeakable strength, the speed of a bullet, and not to mention x-ray vision. You would be thinking that Clark Kent is just a regular everyday guy with far too many weaknesses. It would be like asking yourself if you could beat Superman. You know yourself well enough to know that you don't have a chance against the Man of Steel, but even you could take out Clark Kent.

If you were to ask me who would win a battle between Clark Kent and Superman my answer just might surprise you. I would say, "It just depends on the day, time and the place." Does it shock you that I would say that Clark Kent depending on the circumstances could beat Superman? Let me explain. In this wild journey that we are on called fatherhood, at all times we all want our children to see (Superman) the best in us. But if you are on this journey long enough you will find out no matter how hard you try to hide Clark Kent, who represents our weaknesses, there will be days that our kids will see the worse of us as well.

When my children were born I, like most responsible fathers, dreamed of being everything they needed and more. I was never going to do or allow anything to hurt them. I wanted them to look at their dad and see a hero. I thought that in order to accomplish this that I would have to wear my cape and keep an "S" on my chest at all times. So when my children were born, I locked Clark Kent in a phone booth somewhere and walked around everyday in a Superman outfit. Although there were days that I found the tight leotards to be restricting, the underwear to be uncomfortable, the cool boots to be too big and the cape too heavy. I wore them any way. I had to play the role. After all my children needed a Hero.

After a while the strangest thing started to happen. There were days that my children looked to the sky saw me flying and said, "Look it's a bird?" "No it's a plane?" "No it's dad (Superman)!" Then soon after they stood in amazement of what I could do they would see me like a comet falling from the sky. Saying, "Look it's a falling star lets make a wish." "No that's a wounded duck." No wait a minute it's dad (Clark Kent)!" Smash! I would come down hard leaving a blaze of smoke and fire behind me. Thinking that I have failed again and that I had to make sure that the kids didn't realize that I was not a super hero, I would try to keep my composure stick my chest out and make sure the wind was blowing just right so that my cape would blow in the wind even in my failures. Only to have my children do or say something funny to let me know that I looked like a clown standing their like a super hero, cape blowing in the wind and a pile of leaves and several other types of debris that I had collected on the top of my head during my recent wipe out. I would stand there and wonder what was so funny. These guys should either show me great admiration because I was a super hero or be totally disappointed because I had failed. I had fallen from the sky. I had let them down. Somehow my children have found out that I am not Superman.

I guess all you have to do is live with me for a day or two and the Clark Kent in me will show up.

Maybe, like me, you too have found out that your family does not always need or even want you to be Superman. Maybe you have found that your family loves Clark as much as they love the Man of Steel. Clark Kent would definitely be more appropriately dressed for some occasions. I am simply saying that your kids don't always want Superman. It's Clark that they invite to their ball game and graduation. It's Clark that they ask to come outside and play with them in the front yard, watch a movie, teach them how to ride a bike, or help them with their home work. Not Superman, but Clark. On days like that, Clark Kent beats Superman. Remember that Clark Kent in a matter of seconds can remove his glasses and become Superman.

When you think about it, timing is what made Superman so great. He knew when to be Clark Kent and when to be Superman. Only when needed would he throw his cape on and save the world. Outside of that he got up everyday put his pants on one leg at a time and went to work just like you and me. We must come to the under-standing that when it comes to fatherhood and being a super hero timing is everything.

Too often we spend our time trying to get our children to fall in love with Superman the perfect heroic father. What we forget is it's easy to love Superman. As men what we really want to know is if they are in love with Clark, that imperfect us. If I can get you to love me as Clark Kent you are going to be really impressed when you see me as Superman. But if you are not impressed with me as Clark then you will eventually be disappointed in me even as Superman. How do you teach your kids to love the Clark Kent in you? You love the Clark Kent in them. You love them in their imperfections, and flaws. You love them when they are super kid and when they are not. You love them the way you want to be loved. Unconditionally.

There are a few things that I have learned in my life as a super hero. One is that wherever Superman (the perfect dad) is Clark Kent (the imperfect dad) is not far away and vice versa, they are one. When you think of the character Superman you also think of Clark Kent. When you think of Clark Kent you also think of Superman. You can't separate the two.

What have my children and God taught me about being a super hero? My children and God have taught me to love the Clark Kent in me, because they do. My Children and God have taught me to forgive the Clark Kent in me, because they have. Thanks for allowing me to pretend to be Superman when you knew that I was just plain old Clark.

What's Your Kryptonite?

He was known as the man of steel, and yet his weakness could be found in a pile of green rocks called Kryptonite. Just like him, we all have a form of Kryptonite in our lives. Kryptonite comes in different packages but it always saps your strength and reminds you of your weakness. What is your Kryptonite? What is your weakness? Is it unbridled anger? Maybe it's an insatiable appetite for drugs and alcohol or an overzealous appetite for success. Or maybe it's that horrible thing or those horrible words that you experienced as a child that has never allowed you to fully love others. Maybe it left you so hurt that now your childhood pain is affecting your adulthood destiny. How about your inability to forgive those who have done wrong towards you. Our Kryptonite are things that have left us emotionally blind, lame, paralyzed, crippled and disabled. What is your kryptonite? Take the time and contemplate this. It's difficult to change unless you recognize that there is a problem. Start changing the things that you can change. You don't have to pass your Kryptonite down to your children.

Give Him His Cape Back

In my travels, I often ask teens an intriguing question: "What if Superman were your favorite hero, and you saw him suffering at the hands of his enemies due to the presence of Kryptonite. The villains have stripped him of his cape. He is trying with every helpless breath to crawl just five yards to recover his cape, the very thing that represents his strength. Without it, he is just a man in tights. With it, he is "The Man of Steel. If he reaches it he could regain his dignity and possibly save the world. What would you do?"

Would you:

A. Dishonor him by mocking and telling him how disappointed you were in him

B. Retrieve the cape for him, put it back around his shoulders and cheer your hero on?

C. Help carry him to the cape so that he could save the world?

D. Put the cape on yourself, fight his enemies, help remove the Kryptonite, and become his trusty side-kick who joins him in saving the world.

Ninety-nine percent of the time most people choose that they would come to the rescue, help or fight along side their hero (answers B,C,D). Bottom line they would help him get his cape back. They made this choice even after they discovered that their hero had a weakness. They still were not willing to allow him to be defeated.

At this point in the meeting, I lead the teens to the revelation that this lame superhero is their own fathers. I asked them why would they rescue Superman by making sure that he got his cape back, yet in regards to our fathers we would rather dishonor and tell them how disappointed we are in them. Then, I challenge the teens by saying, "If we can give Superman his cape back, then we can give our fathers their capes back." This simply means giving them not a second chance but another chance to be the hero of our lives. A

93

second chance means strike two and you're out. Another chance means I will love you the way I want to be loved, unconditionally.

Without question, we as fathers will fail more than twice in our lifetime. So what a blessing when they are not willing to take our capes in those moments but to give it back to us in those moments that the Kryptonite of life strips us of it. I end our session by asking the young people: "Who has ever failed? Who here has ever had to ask for someone's forgiveness? Who here has a little Kryptonite in their life and you found out you have some weakness as well?" By now hands have gone up all across the room. Then I end our time by saying, "Then give your father his cape back. Sure some of you have dads that there is just no way your mom is going to let him have contact with you for your own personal safety. But there are some of you here whose fathers are just missing the mark. They just need to know that they have another chance not a second chance. He needs to know that you won't hold his weakness against him. Most fathers need you to do what you would do for your favorite super hero: Give him his cape back." Kids across the country are accepting this challenge. So we as men need to be prepared to receive our capes back and be the leaders and role models that our children need.

In my past, I would have been someone who would have been guilty of taking my father's cape. Some would say that I didn't take it; he gave it to me when he decided that he wanted nothing to do with me. Whatever the case, I was a person who had laughed, mocked, and stood in disappointment of him until I became a father. Then and only then did I realize the grace that I needed to extend to my own absent father. Not that I was absent or abandoned my children in any fashion or form. Although our Kryptonite was different. I too had weakness and days that I have needed my family to give me my cape back. In those moments I felt some sympathy for my own dad who had spent his life cape-less.

Although I have tried to place this cape back around his neck many times since coming to this realization, my dad has refused. While he has not changed I have. I currently have my own cape to wear. So I choose not to wear his. I will neatly fold it in the closet of my heart and wait for that awesome day that I have the honor of pulling it out and draping it around his shoulders again. I look forward to the day that I can give him his cape back. To all fathers I say, "Although life has knocked you down and exposed your weaknesses, get up! There is somebody out there who wants to give you your cape back."

CHAPTER 8

<u>The Power of The Prodigal</u>

The Prodigal Son (Child)

In order to understand the power of the prodigal father you must first understand the story of the prodigal son. An epic adventure from the bible found in Luke 15: 11-32 unfolds the plight of this rags-to-riches father son relationship.

"There was a man who had two sons.

The younger one said to his father, 'Father, give me my share of the estate.' So he divided his property between them.

"Not long after that, the younger son got together all he had, set off for a distant country and there squandered his wealth in wild living.

After he had spent everything, there was a severe famine in that whole country, and he began to be in need.

So he went and hired himself out to a citizen of that country, who sent him to his fields to feed pigs.

He longed to fill his stomach with the pods that the pigs were eating, but no one gave him anything.

"When he came to his senses, he said, 'How many of my father's hired men have food to spare, and here I am starving to death!

I will set out and go back to my father and say to him: Father, I have sinned against heaven and against you.

I am no longer worthy to be called your son; make me like one of your hired men.'

So he got up and went to his father. "But while he was still a long way off, his father saw him and was filled with compassion for him; he ran to his son, threw his arms around him and kissed him.

"The son said to him, 'Father, I have sinned against heaven and against you. I am no longer worthy to be called your son.'

"But the father said to his servants, 'Quick! Bring the best robe and put it on him. Put a ring on his finger and sandals on his feet. Bring the fattened calf and kill it. Let's have a feast and celebrate.

For this son of mine was dead and is alive again; he was lost and is found.' So they began to celebrate.

What a story of restoration. I wish that every story ended in such a victorious celebration.

Some of us can relate to the joy of this father because we too have had our day of celebration and yet there is still some broken hearted father standing and waiting by the road side hoping that his child will come down that road. He is waiting for his day of celebration. The day that he and his child's relationship is restored.

Definition Of A Prodigal

What does the word prodigal mean? It simply means to be wasteful. So another way of saying the title of these stories is the wasteful child or father. What do we waste? What is the most valuable thing we have and the one thing we can never get back? Time. It must be spent wisely and not wastefully. It must be spent loving, learning and leading. Loving those who are presently around us, learning from those older than us and leading those younger than us. Time should never be wasted in anger, unforgiveness or regret. Time is ticking away are you a prodigal or wasteful man? You have read the story of the prodigal son. Now let me tell you the story of the prodigal or wasteful father.

The Prodigal Father

As emotional as the story of the prodigal son is, the story of the prodigal or wasteful father is even more heart wrenching. While this is not a biblical story meaning that I can't tell you to go to any chapter or verse in the bible. I do believe that this issue was a concern from God when you see the scriptures found in Psalms 68:5 which says, "God is a father to the fatherless...." Psalms 27:10 Though my father and mother forsake me, the Lord will receive me. He knew then that there would be prodigal or wasteful fathers. The story of the prodigal father is very similar and yet different to that of the prodigal son.

"There was a man who had two sons who he had not seen since their childhood. Like a dusty, old keepsake photo album his boys charming smiles were fading and trapped behind the sticky plastic of his mind. Each image of his boys reminding him of the life and relationships that he wishes he had. Reminding him of a better time. A time when Christmas mornings were filled with the parental excitement of pulling out perfectly wrapped gifts and video taping his boys as they, with joy, ripped open each gift like untamed lions. A time when at earliest hours in the morning he heard short choppy sounds of little boys' feet swiftly running towards his bed.

Then suddenly there would be a moment of silence. This only meant that his sons had now taken flight toward his bed and would be landing on his chest at any time. The pain was unbearable and yet the moment was priceless. He missed tucking his boys into bed and the nightly ritual that they had started. Without fail, every night after the boys would jump in bed, he would pull the covers over them nice and snug. Rubbing their head with the affectionate touch of a father he would kiss his boys on the cheek and say, "You are the best thing that ever happened to me." The boys in return would say, "You're the best dad in the world, always have been and always will be." With a smile on his face he would cut off the Mickey Mouse light and slowly close the fine white six paneled bedroom door. Apprehensively walking down the hall to the master bed room where he and his wife slept, he often wiped away tears from his eyes. What his boys did not know was that mom and dad were about to disclose a brutal truth to them. They were about to file for a divorce. Over the years their relationship had demised. In front of their children they tried to put on a good show but even the boys noticed their lack of affection and dishonoring acts towards one another.

After months of wondering if it was their fault and going through mind boggling mental battles as to who they wanted to live with, the day came. Their hearts were ripped out. Their bubble of security had been broken. Mom had won custody of the boys and dad, with his weekly visiting rights, promised the boys that their relationship would not change in any fashion or form. As he left to head to his new home now separate from the boys, he rubbed them on their heads kissed them on the cheek and said, "You boys are the best thing that has ever happened to me." Tears running down their face and trying to be brave little soldiers for their father, in return they replied, "You are the best dad in the world, always have been and always will be." The boys stood and watched as their dad made his way through the court room crowd and disappeared behind the lavish cherry wood court room doors. Their mom tried to comfort them but what she didn't understand was that there are some things in a young man's life that his father can only give to him or teach him.

Initially after the divorce the father did a great job staying in contact with the boys. They spent the night at his house on weekends, went to amusement parks and went to the newest action movies. He even would attend their sporting events. One day the younger son said to his father, "I just want you to know that even though you and mom are not together any more you are still the greatest dad in the world." "Always have been, always will be." "Promise us that you won't leave us." In shock his dad said, "I would never leave you."

Soon after that conversation the father found himself swamped with work and trying to make a new life for himself. It was clear that by his ex-wife's dating actions that she had begun to make a new life for herself. Losing track of his priorities, life and the pursuit of success quickly swallowed him up. He found himself all too often not keeping his word to the boys as to when and what time he was going to pick them up. Leaving them broken hearted and without excuse for his actions. It was becoming clear to them that their phone number was moving down the speed dial list on their father's cell phone. Quickly becoming a professional public success and a private family failure, the father was offered an incredible position with great pay. He was absolutely excited about the job. Thinking finally his hard work had paid off. Sure it cost him everything he loved but it had finally paid off. The only problem with his new job was that it was in another country. It would mean being totally separated from the boys. That's just about as much time as he thought about it and then he took the position.

When he had packed all his things he contacted his boys to let them know the news. The boys still young and yet older than they were when the divorce took place stood once again crying. It felt as if their father was being ripped away from them again. Begging him to stay and not to take the job the father assured the boys that everything would be okay and nothing would change. As much as the boys loved their dad they had heard these words before and found that this was not necessarily the truth. Once again pleading with their father they realized that their words were now falling on death ears. Before he jumped into his car to catch a plane for his new life, he rubbed them on their heads, kissed them on the cheek and said, "You boys are the best thing that has ever happened to me." Tears running down their faces, the once little brave soldiers were now unsure of themselves and their father. As their dad headed towards his car the boys said, "You are the best dad in the world, always have been and always will be." The boys stood and watched as their dad closed the car door, put on his shades and drove away waving and saying, "I will be back soon!" "Remember!" "You're the best thing that ever happened to me!" The boys stood in the middle of the road watching their father's car meander its way through city traffic until it became just a tiny moving dot. Not knowing that two years after divorce, 51% of children in sole mother custody homes only see their father once or twice a year, or never again. They stood in full expectation that their father would return soon.

Soon days, months and then years went by and the boys had not heard from their father. Things on the job seemed to be going well. Their dad was restructuring the organization and sales were going through the roof. Although he missed his boys the affection, affirmation and what seemed to be acceptance that he was getting from his peers and employees seemed to be filling his needs. He thought about calling them but he was slightly embarrassed that he had been so irresponsible as a father. So he decided not to call. Then over time his embarrassment turned into shame. So he did not try to make contact with the boys. After that his shame turned into condemnation. Not long afterwards, condemnation turned into what we call an absentee father. This is what I call a prodigal father.

Many years had gone by. Yet day after day his boys had the same daily routine. They would catch the bus home after school and spend a few minutes standing at the top of the driveway looking down the road to see if this would be the day that their dad would come back to see them. As the school bus would pull away it never failed. A few of their class mates would let down the bus windows pointing their fingers, laughing and shouting, "Move on with your life. Your dad's not coming back." As the bus driver would begin to pull away he would tip his hat towards the boys and wink his eye. It was his small way of encouraging the boys not to give up hope. As the bus drove down the street the boys stood there watching until it turned into a small yellow dot. Making their way to the house the first thing that they would do is check the answering machine. Their excitement would always be rekindled whenever they saw the blinking red light. This meant that someone had left a message. They would push the button in great expectation to hear a message from their dad only to be disappointed. It had been this way for years. The answering machine was always full of reminders of practice schedules and doctor appointments but never dad's voice.

Meanwhile on the other side of the country things were not going so well for dad and his job. The market had changed. The economy was bad and not to mention a few public scandals had hurt their public image. Yet his bosses and his organization still expected him to produce. Not blaming moral and economic issues for the company's problems, they began to point their fingers at him. Slowly they took away his company perks and then it happened. They fired him. Stating that they were down sizing. He was devastated. Everything that he had built had now come tumbling down. The people that he had received this false affection, affirmation and acceptance from were now gone. It was all conditional. It was all based on job performance and what he could do for them. Right then he realized that he was expendable to everyone but his boys that is. Now coming to his senses and feeling remorse for the life that he had lived and the time that he had wasted, with tears in his eyes he now knows that it's time to return home to his boys. Wondering if it was too late or if the boys would even accept him back, fear gripped his heart.

As hard as it was for him to leave home he now realized that it would be even harder to return. In leaving he walked down a road full of embarrassment, shame and condemnation. These were the things that eventually kept him away from his family. Now in returning he was going to have to walk back down that same road and deal with the embarrassment, shame and condemnation.

Not knowing that it would take him years to work through such issues. By the time he got up the guts to make it back home to see his boys they were married and with children themselves. It just so happened that the boys and their families were visiting with their mother that day. For years now she had lived at the same property. She found it hard to leave because the place had so many memories for the boys. Some good and some bad. As they were enjoying the family festivities the children asked for permission to play outside in the front yard. The boys remembering how much fun they had out in the yard growing up gave the children permission. They each rubbed their children on the head, kissed them on the cheek and said, "You're the best thing that ever happened to me." In return the kids simultaneously said to the fathers, "You are the best dad in the world. Always have been and always will be." It never failed to warm their hearts when they heard the kids say that. In that moment they got a glimpse of what their own father many years ago must have felt when they made the same statement to him. It also reminded them of all the time that their prodigal father had wasted. At this point in life it had been so long since they had heard from him that they were not even sure if he was still alive or not.

The boys went back to the indoor family activities while the kids ran wild in the front yard. Competitive games of Simon Says and Duck-Duck-Goose kept them amused. They were having the time of their life in the front yard when they noticed a man standing at the top of the driveway. They had never met him before however he did have a strange resemblance to their fathers. Obeying the words of their parents not to talk to strangers the kids ran towards the house. The oldest boy's daughter in her little sweet, raspy voice called for her father. He quickly came to the door to see what his child needed. The young girl standing on the outside of the screen door and her father standing on the inside points towards the top of the driveway and says, "Daddy! " "There is a strange man standing in the driveway." By now the youngest son had also overheard that there was an issue in the front yard. Like two bears whose cubs were in danger, they both came rushing out of the house. As they stepped into the driveway they noticed a strange man standing at the mouth of the driveway. The youngest boy asked, "Is their anything that we can do to help you sir?" The man replied, " Yes!" "You can forgive me." The oldest son asked, "Are you lost?" The man quickly replied, "I was lost, but now I am found." Still wondering what in the world was going on the boys pulled the kids behind them for protection.

Still standing deep back in the driveway the boys suggested that the man move on. The man then said, "I did that once before and I lost the best thing that ever happened to me." Just to humor the old man the boys asked, "And what is the best thing that ever happened to you?" The man began to walk up the driveway very slowly to show himself not to be of any great harm. It had been so long since his boys had seen him that they could barely recognize him. By the time he made it to the middle of the driveway he was close enough for them to clearly see his face. Then he said, "You boys are the best thing that has ever happened to me." The only person that ever said those words to them was their dad. At that moment the boys realized who this stranger was. It was their prodigal father.

Spending a few seconds staring at one another in disbelief they looked at their father with tears in their eyes. Then there was a long moment of awkward silence. The dad figured that the boys silence meant that they disowned him. Just as he had given up hope of ever winning the hearts of his boys back, the silence was broken when the youngest boy's child asked, "Daddy, who is that man?" Lips quivering, tears racing down his face, her father answered, "That's the greatest father in the world, always has been and always will be." The father in unbelief of the statement of acceptance that his son was still willing to make about him fell to his knees in tears. For years he had longed to hear that statement come out of his boys' mouth again. It was a statement of forgiveness. They not only still called him dad, but they still believed that he was the best dad in the world. He knew that he did not deserve it yet his boys were offering him not a second chance but another chance. Rushing towards there dad the boys rapped their arms around him. Holding one another tightly soon a pool of tears formed at their feet. The boys then both turned around and motioned their children to come. Feeling safe now without fear they ran towards their fathers. Hanging around their legs as if their fathers were jungle gyms. The grandchildren for the first time in their life met their grandfather. That day the family spent the day together for the first time in years. It wasn't that the boys did not have a thousand questions for their dad, but they had resolved in their heart to not waste time. Their father was lost and now he was found.

Plea To The Prodigal

I can not count how many young people that I have met with prodigal or wasteful fathers. Countless numbers of them waiting for their dads to come home. Angry? Yes. Hurt? Yes. Yet willing to give you another not a second chance.

Just like the father in the story there is something that stops dads from returning home. Something more than the other angry parent is stopping you from getting back involved in your son or daughter's life. What is it?

In the story of the prodigal or wasteful father the other parent did not stop her children from being involved with their father. The father remained absent due to his own issues. Prodigal fathers around the world are finding out that as hard as it is to leave home it is even harder to return. In leaving you have to deal with fear, embarrassment, shame and condemnation. These are eventually the same things that keep men away from their families. However on the road back home the fear is heightened, embarrassment deeper, shame and condemnation greater than you ever imagined. Only then do you realize just how far away and wasteful you have been. The good news is that a journey of a million miles begins with one step. You just keep putting one foot in front of the other until love leads you home.

CHAPTER 9

The Power of Love

The Great Commandment

One of the greatest commandments in the bible is: "Love your neighbor as yourself." Who is my neighbor? What does learning to love your neighbor have to do with you loving yourself? And, what does this all have to do with you having a loving relationship with your child? Everything!

The word neighbor means: To be close *by,* friend, near. Who do you know that wants to be closer to you more than your child? Who wants to have a friendship with you more than your child? Who longs to be nearer to you more than your child? The answer to all of these questions is, "No one." Today your child is your neighbor, and God commands that we love them as we love ourselves. The problem is that most times we are doing just that. We are loving our children as much as we love ourselves. What we are finding out is that we don't love ourselves that much. This is causing a problem in the relationships that we have with our kids.

Learning to Love Self

In order for us as men to have healthy relationships with our children we must first have a healthy love for ourselves. What our children don't know is that we only criticize them, because we are so critical of ourselves. We never have any thing good to say about them, because we seldom have anything good to say about ourselves. We make them feel as if nothing they do is ever good enough, because some of us have felt that way about ourselves our entire life. We may not give them eye contact when speaking to them, because we don't want to take a good look at ourselves in the mirror of life. A generation is hurting because we are loving them as we love ourselves.

Once I love myself and have a better self image, then not only will I protect them from outside danger, but I would protect them from me. I won't only jump in front of a moving car for my child; I will speak softly and lovingly to them while teaching them to drive that car for the first time. Not only will I take a bullet for my children, I will also watch my criticisms knowing that they have the capability to wound them as much or more than any bullet.

There are 3 steps we must take in order to learn to love ourselves.

Be honest with yourself: This a true sign that you are learning to love yourself. You must honestly admit that there are some areas in your life that must change, but overall you do want what's best for your family. You need to be honest and admit that at times your children have suffered from your lack of love of self.

Be patient with yourself: Give yourself grace while learning to love yourself. Stop beating yourself up for failing or not measuring up. As you take each positive step, celebrate the fact that you're not what you used to be. Sooner or later the patience that you are giving yourself will be the patience that you will freely give to your children.

Begin affirming yourself: Maybe you have never had anyone in your life give you affirmation. Your kids may not understand that. All they know is that you are their dad and that they need affirmation from you. For some reason you never give it to them. It hurts them and makes them feel as if they are not important. They will spend their lives doing things to try to impress you. They just want to hear you say, "Great job" or "I am proud of you." Once you are comfortable giving yourself some affirmation it won't be as hard to give it to others.

I know that this sounds crazy, but occasionally pat yourself on the back. Tell yourself what you longed to hear someone else say. It's okay to tell yourself that you did a great job. Take a look in the mirror as you're brushing your teeth and compliment one of your physical features. Tell yourself that you have the world's greatest smile. It doesn't have to be true to anyone but you.

When you're done doing all these things and you begin to feel differently about yourself, take inventory of how much better your relationship is with your children. You will find that you are once again loving them as you love yourself. The only difference is now you have learned to love yourself in a healthy way thus you can love your children in a healthy way.

What is Love?

While there are many definitions of love, I think the definition found in the bible gives us the best example of love. I Corinthians 13:4-8 reads:

Love is patient, love is kind. It does not envy, it does not boast, it is not proud.

It is not rude, it is not self-seeking, it is not easily angered, it keeps no record of wrongs. Love does not delight in evil but rejoices with the truth. It always protects, always trusts, always hopes, and always perseveres. Love never fails.......

When our children are saying that they need love from us, they are saying that they need patience, kindness etc....To make sure that your child is loved you may have to ask them for their own personal definition of what love is, a written sentence or paragraph. Sounds crazy but it works. At times you may need to go back and revisit the list or definition. Why? Because what you will find out is that with time a person's needs and thus their definition can change. At one point in time your child may need lots of affirmation. Your child makes this known to you and you take appropriate action. You spend the next five years affirming your child to the point that they are healthy in that area. Now their definition or need has changed. They are a teenager who dresses quite strangely so you think. However they convince you that it is not just a phase but it is who they are.

They make it known that at this point in life it is very important for you to accept them for who they are.

As people live and learn their personal definition of love may change. This is why it is important to have them redefine what is love to them. When it comes to love the only thing that won't change are the things that you see in God's word 1Corinthians 13:4-8. Love will always be patient and kind. It will never be envious, boastful, proud, rude, self-seeking, easily angered, keeping record of wrongs, delighting in evil. It will always protect, trust, hope, and persevere. It will never fail. These things are nonnegotiable. So if you are not sure of what your child's needs are always ask for their definition. And always follow the model of love found in God's word.

The Power of Love

His name was Derrick Redmond. It was his childhood dream to be an Olympic athlete and after many years of hard work, sweat, blood and tears he was finally there. The 1992 Barcelona Olympics would be the stage that he would display to the world his unspeakable speed. He was going to prove all the critics wrong. With the eye of a tiger he glared at his opponents as they performed their calisthenics. Everyone of them hoping to somehow intimidate him. The Official made a call for all contestants to take their places. Like a well tamed lion he entered into his starting blocks and waited for the line judge to shoot off the gun. Shouting at the top of his lungs the line judge said, "Runners!" Derrick's blood was pumping he was ready to go. Thousands were watching the race live and millions were at home watching on television. Derrick was ready to shock the world. The Official continued his cadence by raising his gun towards the sky screaming, "Set!" At that moment every runner arched their backs and leaned their weight on their finger tips. Within a blink of an eye they all heard the gun go off. This meant go. Like stallion horses they exploded from the blocks. Muscles rippling, arms under control and yet flailing. The next four hundred meters were going to tell the world who the best man on the track was, so they all thought. Trying to build up speed as quickly as possible. They were all running neck and neck. Then slowly but surely the crowd began to get thinner as some contestants found it harder to keep up as the race picked up speed. The crowd was going wild. Cameras were flashing giving off the semblance of expensive fire works. The elite runners were beginning to pull away from what now was a dwindling crowd. Derrick Redmond was right in the heat of things. Running toe to toe, with the world's best. As the race continued Derrick's confidence was growing. He was stride for stride with the front of the pack and he knew that he had not even kicked into his fastest gear yet.

He would stay the course and run his race. Derrick had a plan. He would wait until just about the half-way mark and then turn on the speed and win the gold. By now all of his friends and family there at the Olympics or back at home are on their feet rooting for him at the top of their lungs. But more than anyone there was one voice that rooted for Derrick that drowned out all others. It was the voice of his father.

Just a few more strides and Derrick would spring his plan upon his opponents. Like an unsuspecting bystander they would be ambushed. For the rest of the race they would have a clear view of the back of his head and the bottom of what his track cleats looked like.

Now in a small pack of elite runners it was time to implement his plan. Like a race car he revved up his engines, kicked into his fastest gear, squalled his tires and begins to leave the other runners in a sea of smoke. As Derrick pulled out to the front of the crowd, those rooting for him screamed even louder. He was winning. Then the unthinkable happened.

A sharp pain ran through the back of Derrick's leg and then he felt something explode. Abruptly disrupting his stride, he reached for the back of his leg and fell helplessly to the ground. Clearly in pain and unable to get back to his feet, the other contestants, like Lear Jets, sprinted past him. In a fraction of a second he was now in last place. Derrick had pulled his hamstring. Not only would he not accomplish his dream of winning the race, he possibly would not even cross the finish line.

The next scene to be played out at the 1992 Barcelona Olympics would become its defining moment. In the midst of the roar of the crowd and the agony of a great athlete, the most unthinkable thing happened. A strange man comes out of the crowd and runs toward Derrick Redmond. At first like everyone else you are wondering how it is possible that this gentleman made it past the high level security at the Olympics and made it onto the track. Your second thought is that someone should get this maniac before he hurts Derrick. Then like the rest of the world you come to the saving knowledge that this man is Derrick's father.

At this point Derrick stands to his feet and he tries to finish the race. His face etched with pain and drenched in tears he falls back to the track. He stands to his feet one more time and starts trying to hop his way down the track. With every effort the viewers groaned as if they could feel his pain.

Just then his dad ran over to Derrick and tried to help him. Not knowing who it was initially Derrick pushed him away. He was determined to make it on his own. At that point Derrick heard a familiar voice say, "Son it's me." Derrick was just as surprised as the rest of the world to see his father down on the track.

He told his father that he had to finish the race and his father's reply was, "Then we will finish the race together." For the next two hundred and fifty meters the world witnessed the power of love. Derrick's father put his arm around his son and step by step, hop by hop they began to make their way towards the finish line.

As they made their way down the track. The entire stadium as well as every one who was at home watching on television stood to their feet and began to applaud them both. Not only were Derrick and his dad crying but every viewer as well. When they finally crossed the finish line it was as if time stood still. The crowd's applause grew even louder and Derrick threw his arms around his father. He did it. He crossed the finish line. He didn't finish first, but he finished.

At the beginning of the race Derrick wanted to show every one in the arena who was the best man on the track. Now he and the rest of the world knew. The best man on the track was the man who came out of the stands and helped his son cross the finish line. The best man on the track at the 1992 Olympics was Jim Redmond, Derrick's father.

What can we learn about love and fatherhood from Derricks' dad? We learn that in life our children will have many finish lines. Finish lines are simply dreams. There will be many finish lines to cross and our children need to know that they don't have to always finish first, sometimes they just need to finish. Our children also need to know that as they are heading towards the finish line of their dreams that there may be obstacles. If they should happen to stumble and fall and life seems to knock them out of the race, like Derrick Redmond's father, we will be in the stands cheering them on. And when things get too bad, they can count on us coming out of the stands to carry them across the finish line. That's the power of love.

CHAPTER 10

The Fight of Your Life

Worth Fighting For

Now that you know what love is, it's time to fight for it. You've got to fight to maintain it. Anything worth having is worth fighting for. It is your job, as a mentor, to help your children success-fully cross each major obstacle (finish line) they encounter in their life. Remember, you lead not only by words but by example.

If you are a distant or absent dad, then the first obstacle your children will have to cross is you. This means that you will have to work on yourself, conquer your own fears, heal from your past, and start a new future. Ok, I know that you may not have had a mentor. Maybe your dad did not show you love. Maybe he was there but disrespectful, nasty and uncaring. This has left you clueless. Sometimes, you feel like you are shooting in the dark. Maybe you have messed up so badly that you don't think that there is a chance that your children would want you back. But the first thing you must do is to **show consistent love** to your children. Keep fighting no matter how they respond to you. In the last chapter, Derrick initially pushed his father away during the race. However, at the end of the race, Derrick needed his father's strength to finish it. Your children may not accept you initially. This is because you may have been inconsistent and uncaring, but if you keep fighting and don't give up, your children will eventually forgive and move on, just like you did from your past.

Now, I know that some men reading this book are great dads, and you're thinking, "What do I have to fight for?" Sometimes, great dads have to fight to maintain relationships with their children as they grow older. Your little girl that you know and love now becomes a preteen. She states that you don't understand her. Better yet, she's dating a jerk that does not treat her as well as you do. How about your son? He wants to be cool and realizes that you don't fit that definition (cool). Now all of a sudden, you don't know who your kids are. Well, it's time to fight. NO, it's not time to fight your kids. It's time to **fight to get to know your kids**. Fight to find out what makes them tick. What makes them happy? What makes them feel loved? You must become a detective. No, I don't want you to sneak through their property and read their diary. I want you to study them. Ask them how you can meet their needs as a father. And without compromise of your standards and beliefs, help to direct and encourage them.

All fathers need to make sure that they are **leading first by example**. Ask yourself, how do you treat their mother? The mother needs to be treated with respect whether you are married, estranged or legally separated. This is important for both sons and daughters. This will help your daughter to know what type of man to choose and will direct your son on how to treat women. Next, make sure that you spend quality time with your children. I think that taking your children on a date/outing separately and as a group builds relationship and trust. My children also see me take my wife on dates. I currently do this with my daughters. I take them out. I buy them something. I make them feel special so that each of my girls knows how they should be treated.

The average daily amount of one-to-one father/child contact reported in this country is less than 30 minutes a day. One of the greatest mistakes dads make is to think that it's the mother's job to build and maintain relationships with the children, especially when the children are young. One day the dad looks up and he does not know his own kids. He was so busy making a living and keeping the family financially stable that his children are starved for affection from their dad. No matter how old your children are, one month old or 15 years old, you've got to **get involved**. Start changing diapers or start spending time with your children.

Next, during this fight you've got to be able to **say "I'm sorry."** Look, for every child you have, you are a first time father for that individual child. This means that just because your first child thrived from your great fatherly skills doesn't mean your second child will respond to the same approach. That means that mistakes will happen. And, most likely they will happen quite often. Therefore, being apologetic is very important and necessary. When you apologize, you've got to really mean it. So, the absent father will apologize for his absence. He will make efforts to start seeing his children more consistently. The inconsistent father will apologize for disappointing his children and will only make promises that he can keep. Most fathers should apologize for letting their past affect their children. After apologizing, make a change.

Some of you are saying, "Why should I apologize? I did the best that I could do." Or better yet, you say, "I did better than what my dad did." Yes, I recognize that most of us did or are doing our best. But sometimes your past mentors including your dad, should not be your standard. Maybe your dad was a very bad father. Man up! And consider apologizing. Your kids need you.

I'm sure you have figured out by now that the older your kids are the harder it is for them to accept your apology. Small kids will forgive quicker than older adult children. And, some kids naturally forgive and it takes others longer. However, if you fight hard and be consistent you will find that most children young and old want to have a dad.

If you don't fight for your kids then who will? You can't expect your children to fight. They are still kids. And, if they are adults, they still will be waiting for you to **make the first move**. It's scary to make the first move. Most men don't like to admit that they are scared. It's better to play macho man than to admit you are scared. This is not the time for that. Don't let your fears control you. This is one of the biggest challenges of your life. This is bigger than the homecoming game. This is bigger than getting a promotion. This is the legacy you will leave behind. You are the example for them.

Now is the time. If not now, then when? Tighten up your chin strap. Leave it all on the field. It's time to man up. It's time to fight and **WIN**.

The Power of a Paper Plate

He wasn't sure what happened. His fifteen year old boy had changed. He was no longer the spunky, curly headed, admiring son he once knew. Now he was angry, secretive and disrespectful. The relationship between Dwayne and his son had taken a turn for the worst.

Some time went by and Dwayne never felt further from his son. It seemed no matter what they were talking about it turned into in argument. Every spoken word was just another opportunity to express their frustrations. At times it even seemed as if Dwayne's son Joe was out making bad choices just to spite his father.

Afraid of the road that his son was heading down Joe's father made countless attempts and pleas to try to rebuild their relationship. He tried the one on one father son talks and every other known strategy to man. He did everything he knew to do to try to reach his son. Joe was non-responsive. As a matter of fact Dwayne and Joe had recently gotten into a huge argument that left Dwayne questioning his fathering skills and left Joe quietly vowing in his heart never to talk to his dad again.

Greatly discouraged Dwayne was not sure what to do to reach his son or how to communicate his feelings for him. It seemed that all would be lost. In one more attempt to fight for the heart of his son Dwayne decided to write Joe a letter.

Not able to find an appropriate piece of paper or words that day Joe's dad grabbed a paper plate and began to write. At first like any man it was difficult to express himself. But with each word he wrote he found it a little bit easier to communicate his thoughts. A few sentences and a lot of misspelled words later Joe's dad signed off, "Love dad."

Putting his pen down and strategically placing that paper plate on the table he headed for work that day. Dwayne had no idea just how powerful the words on that paper plate would be. Time would only tell.

That morning his son Joe got up and went through the typical teen routine in getting ready for school. After he got himself together he headed downstairs to eat some breakfast. In a hurry Joe decided to grab something that he could take with him.

Joe then picked up his book bag and headed towards the front door. As he walked past the dining room table he noticed a paper plate that had his name written on it. He could tell by the messy hand writing that it was his father's penmanship. Figuring that his father was probably making plans to send him off to some kind of military school he decided to take a peep.

Joe picked up the paper plate and began to read. At first he was very defensive. Then slowly but surely he could feel his anger subside. Soon his lips started to quiver and tears filled his eyes. He tried to fight his emotions but it was too late. The words that his father wrote on that paper plate were profound. That day Joe's heart melted and he cried for the first time in years.

On that Paper plate Dwayne simply expressed his love for his son. He let Joe know how much he loved him. He apologized for the times that he did not express that love well. He let Joe know that he believed in him and that someday Joe would grow up and do something great.

From that day on Dwayne and Joe's relationship began to heal. They have a wonderful father son relationship now. But, only because Dwayne was willing to fight for his son.

Many years later Joe grew up to be all that his father wrote on that paper plate and more. Joe grew up and worked with the largest young adult led ministry in the world. By the age of twenty he had spoken to thousands of struggling teens across the United States. Dwayne could not have been more proud than to see his little boy grow up and change the world.

For over ten years Joe has managed to hold on to that paper plate. When he traveled across America speaking to troubled youth he had that paper plate with him. When he got married and became the father of two, he had that paper plate with him. Who would have ever imagined that a paper plate could be so powerful?

It brings new meaning to the term full plate. Not full of edible food. But a plate full of love.

Joe's dad fought for his son with a paper plate and it worked. Let me ask you, "How many paper plates do you have?" What are you willing to do to win your child's heart?

CHAPTER 11

<u>Following & Fighting</u>

Following His Father's Foot Steps

He was just three years old on that unforgettable day. Now seventeen he remembers it like yesterday. His dad reached over and straightened out his wrinkled collar as they walked down to the local candy store.

It was always typical for people to honk horns or wave at his father as they walked down the street. In their city his dad was a known hero to some and to others a menace. Simply put he was a drug dealer.

The honking horns and waving hands was not all that was common for them as they walked down the street. It was also common for his dad to take two or three steps and then take a quick suspicious look behind him. Most times it was even hard for them to have an eye to eye talk because his father was too busy looking over his shoulder.

Everyone thought that his dad was a tough guy but he knew differently. He knew that his father was paranoid about more than just the cops catching him and spending time in prison. His father was afraid that someone might get him before the cops did. So he spent his life looking over his shoulder.

They had made it a few blocks before his father found out that the thing he feared most was in front of him and not behind him. Two guys that he thought were friends and or admirers were headed in his direction. Being familiar with them it never crossed his mind that he or his son was in danger. After all they were from the same neighborhood. He supplied these guys with drugs to make money as well.

As they got closer to the two young men. His father walked a few steps ahead of him and shouted out his streetwise words acknowledging his friends presence. He reached in his pocket. Then he stretched out his hand in their direction to give them what always seemed to be a secret hand shake. There was nothing secret about it except for the fact that as the hand shake took place drugs and money would quickly be passed from one person to the other. Then both parties would hastily keep moving in opposite directions. It looked like a simple hand shake but it was really a drug deal.

This time was different. When his father put his hand out. One of the two young men reached in his pocket as if he was going to pull out money to pay for the drugs. Instead he pulled out a gun.

With very little time to react. Within a spilt second his father turned back towards his son and began to run. Now with his son in front of him shots ring out. The noise was so deafening that the little boy quickly and fearfully threw his hands over his face.

At that moment the boy heard the two young men take off running and people in the neighborhood screaming. Removing his now bloody hands from his face he saw his father standing wearily before him. Covered in blood his dad was looking directly at him. For the first time in his three-year-old life his dad was not looking over his shoulder to see what was behind him. He was looking at what was in front of him. His son. Eye to eye.

The boy's last memory of his father would be, his father falling on top of him and bleeding to death of gun shot wounds. There he laid crying and being crushed by his father's half warm body.

Within minutes neighbors had made it to his home and informed his mother of her husband's horrible fate. Running down the street to the crime scene she panicked when she saw her husband's body on the ground. She panicked even more when she saw her little boy trapped underneath his father. Not sure if he had been shot as well. She carefully pulled him from underneath his dad and took him to safety.

Even though he was just three years old. His father's death and how he died would be a defining moment in his life.

To some of you this story may sound too horrific to be true. Nonetheless it is the sad but true story of a young man that I met in my travels. His name was Shane.

I was invited to speak to a group of young men and women who were spending time in a high security juvenile detention center. Some were there for heinous crimes and others for petty ones. Yet they all had done the crime and were serving the time.

I shared my story and my plight of fatherlessness because I knew that over 70% of juveniles in state operated institutions have no father. By the end of my speech there were very few dry eyes in the building. It seemed as if every kid in the room wanted to talk afterwards. So I asked the leadership if I could have a supervised room where I could talk with kids in private. They agreed and as each kid walked in the room a gut wrenching story followed them.

It was not that any of these teens' stories were more important than the others, but I will never forget Shane's story. Shane walked into the room with tears in his eyes. And I noticed although we were at a juvenile detention center every few steps he took he looked over his shoulder to see if someone was following him.

It didn't take long for Shane to open up and tell me about his life and the death of his father. Then I asked him a very important question. I asked Shane why was he incarcerated. Shane paused wiped the tears out of his eyes and said,

"I am a drug dealer and I got busted for selling drugs."

Somewhat thrown back by what he said I asked him to repeat himself. Shane gave me the same unbelievable answer. He was a drug dealer. After all that drugs had done to destroy his life, stealing away any opportunity to know his father, watching his dad be murdered, and having his father die on top of him. Shane still thought that selling drugs was the way to go.

I asked Shane why he would get involved in a life style that took so much away from him in such a horrible way. Shane still crying replied that it was all he had left of his dad. It was the road that his father left for him to walk. He greatly missed his father and the only way that he felt close to him was to follow in his foot steps. He wanted to be like his dad. Even if it meant dying like his dad.

I asked Shane if he was ready to spend the rest of his life looking over his shoulder. He gave no comment. I asked Shane if he desired to get married and have children someday himself? He said yes. I asked Shane does he want to die on top of his child some day. Shane said no. I ended our conversation with challenging Shane to find some other set of foot prints to follow.

Like Shane's dad we as men spend to much time looking at what's behind us and not focusing enough on what is in front of us. Of course not all of us are drug dealers but the cares and worries of this life can lead us to spend too much time looking over our shoulder to see what's behind us. What's behind us? The past, failures and mistakes are behind us.

What's in front of us? Our kids. Our future and our legacy. If Shane's father had known that his son would one day grow up to follow in his footsteps, that one day he might be murdered in front of his child and die on top him, I would say that Shane's father, even though a drug dealer, would never want that for his son.

Shane's dad spent his life looking behind him and in the last seconds of his life he looked in front of him and saw his son. It was too late. He had left a road of foot prints that his child would choose to follow.

You say but I am not a drug dealer. I would ask are you an alcoholic, angry person, workaholic, impatient, unforgiving, critical, physically abusive, verbally abusive, not paying attention to your children, unapproachable, non communicative? Then you are laying footprints that will soon be followed.

Jacob Is Still Wrestling

I like to refer to this generation of young people as the Jacob Generation. It may sound strange at first but it makes perfect sense when you know the story of Jacob. The Jacob story is found in the old testament of the bible, the book of Genesis chapter 27-32 is what we will focus on.

Jacob was the youngest of twin brothers. His older brother Esau was not only totally opposite of Jacob but he was next in line to receive his father's blessing. It seemed as if Esau at all times had his father's attention. At least he thought that they had more in common. For years Jacob longed for his father's favor, his blessing, his attention.

As Jacob's father got older in years and was on his death bed he asked to see his oldest and what seemed to be his favorite son, Esau, so that he could bless him before he passed away. While Esau was preparing a special meal for him and his father, Jacob and his mother came up with a plan.

Once again always longing for the blessing and attention of his father, Jacob decided to steal his brother's blessing. He decided to dress up as his brother and fool his father. He even went as far as to make the same meal that his father had requested his brother to make. Then he put on some of Esau's clothing so that he would look and smell like his brother. Finally because his brother was hairier than two timber wolves, Jacob took goatskins and covered his hands and his neck. This was just in case his father touched him.

Considering the fact that Jacob's father had poor eyesight his plan worked. Surely enough his father gave him his brother's blessing. Jacob fought and stole his brother's blessing. You don't have to agree with how he got the blessing nonetheless he was blessed.

Later in life Jacob would once again find himself fighting for another blessing. Only this time it would be with Father God.

Sending his family ahead of him in his journey he found himself alone. The bible tells us that at that moment God showed up and began to wrestle with Jacob. After much wrestling God said to Jacob, "Let me go!" Jacob's reply was, "I will not let you go unless you bless me." God then asked Jacob a question, "What is your name?" Jacob answered and said, "Jacob." Then God said, "Your name will no longer be Jacob, but Israel……" That day Jacob fought and God blessed Jacob.

This generation of teens reminds me of Jacob for many different reasons. They constantly feel as if they are next in line and never the first in line to get a blessing from their fathers. There is always something that gets their father's attention just a little bit more than they do.

Because Esau seemed to have his father's attention and his blessing, Jacob was never content with himself. The Jacob generation is the same way. We have not told them that we love them for who they are and who God has created them to be. So our kids grow up trying to be like Esau. They dress, smell and act like Esau all just to try to get our attention, our blessing. We have somehow made them feel that to just be Jacob is not good enough. Like Jacob this generation for years have longed for their father's favor, blessing and attention. And they have been fighting for it.

How have they fought for my blessing you ask? Well some times they fight for it by acting out in rebellious ways. If you listen quietly and read between the lines you will hear them simply saying, "Daddy will you bless me?" On the outside they are communicating that they want you to stay away from them, but trust me the inside is screaming something totally different. The inside is shouting, "Bless me." Pay attention to me, tell me who I am, give me an identity.

Even as Jacob finds himself wrestling with God it is still the same picture of a young man fighting with his source, authority figure and or covering to get a blessing. Only this time he doesn't have to steal it.

Here is Jacob wrestling for a blessing from God. The bible tells us that he put up a pretty good fight. God demanded that Jacob let him Go. Jacob said, "Not until you bless me." He was saying not until you give me a blessing that I don't have to steal. Not until somebody blesses me for just being me. Not until somebody tells me that being Jacob is enough.

Then God read between the lines of this little feisty creation called Jacob. He asked Jacob what his name was and Jacob told him. It was not that God didn't know his name but he was doing a work inside of Jacob. He needed Jacob to accept who he was before he could become who he wanted to be.

That night God changed Jacob's name. Not only did he change his name he changed his identity. He changed his life.

Our young people today are wrestling with us as Jacob wrestled with God. As a whole we as men have treated them as if we want them to let us go. I am busy right now, let me go. I will make it to your game next week, let me go. We'll catch that movie tomorrow, let me go. Meanwhile our kids are wrestling with us for a blessing and saying, "I will not let you go until you bless me." "Please bless me, tell me who I am, pay attention to me, and tell me that I am enough." They are begging for us to say something that will change their name, identity, and their lives. Jacob is still wrestling.

What does the youth of this nation want? They want to hear us say, "Jacob you can stop wrestling. The fight is over. Your father is paying attention. You are enough. Your father desires to bless you. You don't have to keep trying to be Esau. You are no longer next in line but you are now at the front of the line.

Why would we move our children to the front of the line? Because we now understand that we as fathers possess a God given divine power. It is called the power of dad.

Final Thoughts

The Unappreciated Dad

You spend every passing moment that you possibly can with your child. You have made or turned down defining career moves because you have placed your children in high priority. You haven't missed a ball game, recital, school play or awards ceremony in fifteen years. You are a great dad.

Every Father's Day your family buys you another neck tie or Bill Cosby sweater that looks like the one they got you the year before. As a matter of fact one entire side of your closet is totally dedicated to neck ties and Bill Cosby sweaters. The sad part is that your children expect you to wear this stuff and wear it often.

You very seldom hear statements like I love you, thank you or you're the greatest. Your children just assume that you are a dad and this is what dads do. Little do they know how blessed they are to have a dad like you that is willing to go above and beyond the call.

You wouldn't tell anyone this, but sometimes you wonder if you even matter. It seems that all you do goes unnoticed. You feel as if you are invisible unless some one in the house needs something or something in the house breaks. And even on those days you are their second choice. Because the truth is that they would much rather have Dr. Phil and Tim the Tool Man deal with these issues. But since they were not available they figure you'll have to do.

If this sounds familiar to you then you may be suffering from Unappreciated-dad-i-tis syndrome. Simply put you are a dad that feels unappreciated. You need to know that there are thousands of responsible fathers who feel the exact same way that you do. You are not alone. The renowned preacher, Billy Graham, put it in these words, **"A good father is one of the most unsung, unpraised, unnoticed, and yet one of the most valuable assets in our society."**

Yes you are a father and sure there are things that all dads should just do. You should even be willing to go beyond and above the call. Is it wrong to desire an, I love you, thank you or you're the greatest sometime? No. What we need to keep in mind is that our kids don't realize that we, like them at times, need acceptance, affirmation and appropriate affection from them as well. You can try to deny this but there isn't a man in his right mind who wants his kids to hate him, never touch him and or never say, "I love you."

What we men have to remember as we run this race called fathering is that this is a long distance race and not a sprint. And like any race that you have ever participated in the **trophies are given out at the end of the race**. All the awards are given out after you cross the finish line. Not before and not during but after. No I love you, thank you or you're the greatest. We just keep running until we see and cross the finish line. We must keep in mind that with every step that we take we are fighting and running for our children.

Where is the finish line? As long as we are alive we are our child's father, defender and protector. Our finish line is our funeral. Not that it is the only time that I would like to hear loving words from my children. But nothing will be greater than to have your children stand at your funeral and say, "Here lies the greatest father in the world. Always has been, always will be."

That's when you will know that your 500 year plan has been released in the earth. What 500 year plan? That plan to touch the next 500 generations of your family. You never know how far out the results of the life you are living could possibly have on your family tree. This kind of powerful effect can only be done through the power of God and the power of dad. It can only be done through the God given influence that God has given every father too positively or negatively affect their children. So choose this day how you will use the power you have as a dad.

About The Author

B rian Pruitt is the Founder and CEO of Brian Pruitt Motivational.

Brian is an international Motivational Speaker who inspires youth and adults to overcome obstacles and accomplish their dreams.

Brian Graduated from Central Michigan University in 1995 with a Bachelor's Degree in Communications. A gifted athlete, Brian Played football for CMU and in 1994 was named AP First Team All American. He has subsequently been inducted into the CMU Sports Hall of Fame. He has also been inducted into the Saginaw County Hall of Fame in Saginaw, Michigan.

Mr. Pruitt has traveled across this country and others challenging and teaching listeners to overcome obstacles and accomplish their dreams. In addition, he has been a regional presenter for Youth Alive-7 Project, and has been featured guest on several television programs. Brian has been honored as a key note speaker for well known ministries such as Teen Mania. He has served as a Motivational Speaker and Life Coach for youth, adults, church's, sports teams, and businesses throughout the U.S, Canada, Mexico, and Sweden.

As an Author, Successful Entrepreneur, and Television Personality Brian's message is reaching the world and igniting passion. Brian and his wife, Delicia have been married for over twelve years and have two daughters, Brianna Joy & Destiny Danae. They reside in Saginaw, Michigan.

<u>Brian Pruitt Motivational Product Promotional</u>

If you have enjoyed reading The Power of Dad then you will love:

The Power of Dad Workbook

Great for:
Individual Devotional Time
Men's Small Groups
Leading Men's Retreats

You've come this far now finish the journey!

The Power of Dad Workbook can only be bought at Brian Pruitt Motivational. Go to our web site located at <u>www.haccman.com</u> or call us at (989) 249-0951

Click on our products link. We will ship The Power of Dad Workbook out and you will have the tools that you need to continue to take the men in your community deeper.

If you are wondering yes Brian Pruitt has other great Books, CD's, DVD's, and Clothing for youth and adults alike. <u>www. haccman.com</u>

Contact Brian Pruitt to speak at your next event.

If you would like Brian Pruitt to come and speak at your next event here are a few ways to contact us. Brian is great for
Corporate Meetings
Church's
Colleges
School Assemblies
Sports Teams
Men's Conferences
Youth Conferences
You name it! Brian Pruitt Motivational is your fit.

Address:
Brian Pruitt Motivational
P.O. Box 294
Saginaw, MI 48606

Phone: (989) 249-0951

E-Mail: brianpruitt41@hotmail.com
Or contact@haccman.com

To find out more about Brian Pruitt Motivational please go to our web site.

WWW.HACCMAN.COM

Printed in the United States
148050LV00001B/29/P

9 781604 775914